Memoirs of a Medicine Man

Memoirs Of A Medicine Man

What Medical School Forgot To Mention

Ernest W. Abernathy, M.D.

1663 Liberty Drive, Suite 200
Bloomington, Indiana 47403
(800) 839-8640
www.AuthorHouse.com

This book is a work of non-fiction. Unless otherwise noted, the author and the publisher make no explicit guarantees as to the accuracy of the information contained in this book and in some cases, names of people and places have been altered to protect their privacy.

© *2005 Ernest W. Abernathy, M.D. All Rights Reserved.*

No part of this book may be reproduced, stored in a retrieval system, or transmitted by any means without the written permission of the author.

First published by AuthorHouse 08/01/05

ISBN: 1-4208-5705-3 (sc)
ISBN: 1-4208-5704-5 (dj)

Library of Congress Control Number: 2005904561

Printed in the United States of America
Bloomington, Indiana

This book is printed on acid-free paper.

For
Mary

DEDICATION

This book is dedicated to the patients
who granted me the privilege and the honor
to be of service to them in more than
7,000 hospital surgeries,
688,000 office visits

FOREWORD

The practice of medicine or surgery is not just sore throats, colds and the flu, removing gall bladders, back aches or belly aches. It is, however, a roller-coaster cornucopia of people and events where drama, comedy, the heights of joy and the depths of sadness are only moments away, as if a revolving door is constantly ejecting the next encounter—a child with appendicitis, a broken arm, the Ku Klux Klan with death threats, gunshot wounds, snake handlers, con artists, sex, racism, rape, a sweet old lady with arthritis, or some addict—a never-ending myriad.

Thankfully, most of my patients and I grew old together in an air of love and mutual respect, in an era of closeness between patients and doctors, when doctors really cared not only about the patient's health, but also about the patients themselves.

Medical school forgot to mention ethics, or talk about humanistic qualities, abstract values outside the world of science. The patient is not just a patient case, (that "gallbladder" in room 911), or a number, but is a unique human being, with emotions, feelings, worthiness, fears, hopes and worries, as well as the capabilities of understanding and courage in the face of disaster. He or she deserves full respect.

"Ten Years of Rape," "Green Door of Racism," "Save A Sexist and Lose A Patient," and "The Comedy Corner" are true stories about the people who traverse these pages, a few of the curious encounters in my forty-year love affair with helping people—sometimes called the practice of medicine.

TABLE OF CONTENTS

Dedication	vii
Foreword	ix
Physician's Prayer	xiii
The Silver Llama	1
A Tender Story	9
The Green Door Of Racism	14
The Hockey Stick	22
Charity Hospital Emergency Room—New Orleans	31
Medical Miracle	39
Boudreaux	39
The Legend Known As Tex	43
An Unforgettable Character	43
Ten Years Of Rape	49
Case Of The Egg Girl	49
Case Of The Mall Shopper	52
Case Of The Barbcue Fork And The Narc Agent	54
Case Of The Police Station Rape	55
Case Of A Man Raped	57
Case Of Court Testimony	59
A Different Kind Of Rape	61
Snakehandlers	65
Snakes Case #1: Rattlesnakes And Religion	65
Snakes Case #2: Copperhead	67
Snakes Case # 3: Uncertain Species—Cotton-mouth Moccasin?	70
Snakes Case # 4: "Snake-in-the-grass"	71
Snakes Case # 5: A Fable	71
Rumors	73
Rumor One—The Baptist Bombardiers	74
Danny	77
Rumor Number Two—That Blonde Beautician	78
Rumor Number Three—Doctor "H"—A Malignant Rumor	79
Rumor Number Four—The Beauty Shop	80
A Little Girl	83
Abuse	83
Self-Abuse	86

Save A Sexist And Lose A Patient	*88*
From My File Of Cases:	
Case Of Mr. X (I Shall Call Him Mr. John)—	
One Of My Earliest "Sexist Cases"	*90*
Case Of Mrs. X (I Shall Call Her Joan)—	
A Highly Placed County Official	*92*
Two Cases—Wife-Swapping Parties	*94*
Case Of Miss Y (I Shall Call Her Miss Jane)	*97*
The Voice	*99*
The Comedy Corner	*103*
Jaw-Breakers	*103*
The Interview	*104*
Unusual Names & Words	*107*
Forace	*108*
Smoke	*111*
Pride And Joy-Juice	*112*
S.O.B. Or Not To Be	*115*
A Short Note On Deep South Southernese	*116*
Kitchener	*118*
Bob Hope	*125*
Second Opinions	*129*
The Folly Of Required Second Opinions (RSO's)	*132*
Destiny And Dynamite	*134*
Rose And The Maruyama Vaccine	*140*
Molly's Malady	*144*
The Incompetent	*148*
Mrs. D's Dilemma	*154*
Terrafirmitis	*157*
Orphelia And The Wagon Of Life	*163*
Cloteelia	*167*
Circus Maximus	*173*
Epilogue	*177*

PHYSICIAN'S PRAYER

Thank you, Lord, for the privilege of being a doctor, for letting me serve as Your instrument in ministering the sick and afflicted.

May I always treat with reverence the human life, which You have brought into being.

Keep me constantly alert to see that the sacred right to live is never violated for any individual.

Deepen my love for people so that I will always give myself gladly and generously to those stricken with illness and suffering.

Help me to listen patiently, diagnose carefully, prescribe conscientiously and follow through faithfully.

Teach me to blend gentleness with skill, to a be a doctor with a heart as well as a mind.

— author unknown

To laugh often and much;
to win the respect of intelligent
people and the affection of children;
to earn the appreciation
of honest critics and endure the
betrayal of false friends;
to appreciate beauty;
to find the best in others;
to leave the world a bit better,
whether by a healthy child,
a garden patch or a
redeemed social condition;
to know even one life
has breathed easier
because you have lived.
This is to have succeeded.

— Emerson

THE SILVER LLAMA

It was Christmas Eve, just past midnight. The holiday held little joy for me; I was filled with despair and foreboding because I had reached a sad decision, to give up medicine. My weary footsteps echoed in the darkened, long basement corridor of The Johns Hopkins Hospital as I trudged slowly toward my mailbox in the hospital post office. I was worn out, deeply depressed, and was seriously questioning the validity of my intended future in the world of medicine. I pondered the questions, "Is this goal worth the chase?" Am I a "burnt-out" case already?" The answer was about to slam me in the face. Meanwhile, I brooded.

After completing four years of college pre-med, four more hard years of medical school had been difficult while holding down as many as thirteen different jobs. Some of those jobs had included working at the Ford Motor plant in Atlanta, then driving to Big John's Charbroiled Hamburgers on Highway 42, south of Atlanta, working as a cook until 1:00 A.M., then going in old jalopy to northeast Atlanta to mop and wax the floors at the LaVista Woman's Club from 2:00 A.M. until 4:00 A.M. for $1.00 per hour. After mopping and waxing, I would catch an hour or two of sleep on one of their couches, then head to Grady Memorial Hospital to be there about dawn. Other jobs varied from every fourth to every fourteenth night.

I was accustomed to work. My experiences included being a ditch digger, lumberjack, pipe layer, milkman, house painter, brick mason assistant, postman, common laborer member of the International Brotherhood of Common Laborers and Hod-Carriers, milkman, surgery extern, oxygen therapist, yard man, and typist, all of which bonded me closer to the patients I would eventually see later in life.

It had taken nine years of university to get this far. I was twenty-seven years old and would be completing Internal Medicine at Hopkins in six more months. The time had arrived to commit to four or five more years of specialty training in surgery, which would also commit me to trying to exist during that same period of time in abject poverty, on a salary of $25 per month. My standard of living was already far below the poverty level, and about to become worse for those five additional years. The proverbial church mouse would be as rich as the Rockefellers or the Vanderbilts, if compared to me. Down deep inside this near-fugue state, I was beginning to question making such a commitment.

Christmas spirit? My spirit was dragging the bottom. Sending gifts to my parents and my two brothers had been out of the question, due to the lack of the financial means to do so. Insolvency was the order of the day for me, precluding movies, travel, concerts, or dining out. I was too ashamed to ask my parents for gasoline money in order to visit them during a brief vacation. A nursing student date requested a dinner at a particular restaurant unknown to me. After being seated in the fancy restaurant, a look at the menu startled me. It indicated more that a month's salary would be required just for appetizers. I was embarrassed to admit I could not afford the tariff, but I had no choice. One shrimp cocktail for her and a glass of water for me finished my one and only stab at a night out. There was no money and no time to keep up with what was popular in music or movies.

My former high school and college classmates now had families with nice homes and amenities, good incomes, new automobiles, and a style of comfortable living socially. They were advancing in the business world economically, incomes climbing ever higher, while during the same nine years I was just advancing in knowledge. I realized my classmates would have children in high school by the time I could complete an additional five years of profound poverty, earning only the aforementioned $25 per month. By the time I finished, I would be 32 years old, and just starting. (make that 34 years of age—I was unaware another two years of military service also would be added before I could start) Frankly, I was bitter, filled with envy of my former classmates.

In this forlorn cloud of doom, I chastised myself for having started upon this masochistic, prolonged and seemingly never-ending quest. I had always felt medicine to be a noble calling, dedicated to the benefit of one's fellow man, serving the public as a doctor. (in my case as a surgeon) Four or five more years loomed for me and seemed an insurmountable goal.

The lonely echoes of my steps in the shadowy, dimly-lit hallway only added to my sagging spirit. I had a real case of the "blues." The baby that I had just delivered in a taxi outside the Emergency Room came to mind, and I wondered if someday he would walk these same hallways, deciding *his* future. (Obstetrics was not my responsibility, but no one else had been available at the time. While a medical student at Emory University's teaching hospital, Grady hospital in Atlanta, I had delivered dozens of babies, so I had stepped in where I was needed, in the taxi.)

As I entered the mailroom at Hopkins, my mind had about settled the issue. I was ready to give up, quit the race, drop the baton, and walk away from the world of medical service. A nine-to-five kind of job was what I needed, such as a pharmaceutical company, or an insurance company, something with the immediate gratification of an income and the bonus of time needed to enjoy living a real life, like everybody else. The chase was over. There was to be no holy grail at the end of my rainbow. I had no way of knowing the next moments would change everything.

The tiny mail box for Interns and Resident doctors at Hopkins opened, revealing a crumpled envelope, pinkish, much like the newborn baby I had just delivered. The wrinkled, abused envelope was addressed simply, "*El Senor Doctor Ebernathy*, Johns Hopkins Hospital, Baltimore, Maryland. One lumpy end of the envelope was so heavy, the envelope flopped over and nearly dropped out of my hands. "Curiosity kills the cat," is an old trite expression, but mine had peaked, interest definitely stirred. I opened it carefully.

Oddly enough, once inside, I found a second envelope labeled simply, "*El Senor* Doctor Abernathy, (with an A this time). The first envelope was re-inspected for clues. Aha! There was a postmark, Rochester, Minnesota, home of the famous Mayo Clinic. I questioned, "What's going on here? I don't know anybody in Rochester, Minnesota."

Palpation of the "lumpy part of the envelope" showed the mass within to be quite hard and irregular in form, like a rock or perhaps a small lump of coal. Hmm, coal. Bemused, my thoughts jumped to earlier times when, as small tots, we were told our Christmas gift would be a lump of coal and switches if we had been "bad." I could not imagine what the lump might be. Christmas—surely not a lump of coal.

As I opened the second envelope, the "lump" fell into my hands. To my surprise, it was a small hand-wrought llama of pure silver. The llama is the national animal of Peru. It was crafted entirely of thick silver wiring into a compact, full-bodied silver stature of almost four inches length, and three inches height. A note explained that a friend heading to the Mayo Clinic had been asked to forward the enclosed letter to me. There was in addition an antiqued parchment paper document, in a beautiful, scripted hand of flowing cursive penmanship. The text was written in the form of a testamentary, with a large official seal near the bottom, signed twice, and embossed upon a formal sealing of wax stamped with an official family crest. My interest now was like a fully accelerating rocket on July fourth.

The document was signed by two wonderful people whom I recalled instantly, the General of the Air Force of Peru and his beautiful wife. My eyes began to tear as I read their expressions of eternal gratitude to me for the part I had played in saving his life. It had happened a few months previously, during a critical moment of emergency in his illness. The language of the document was graceful and eloquent, detailing the circumstances of my participation in his recovery. As I read, some of those tears began to course down my face.

The entire incident came immediately to mind. The General came to The Johns Hopkins Hospital because he was suffering severely from an illness called Malignant Hypertension. In 1959, this illness was usually fatal within one year, during which the blood pressure would soar to uncommon and extremely high levels, the patient would become permanently blind, and die of heart attack, a "stroke," or kidney failure. The General had progressed to the point that he had already lost most of his sight. Despite medications, his blood pressure was 240 over 160, extremely high and dangerous. He was imminently in danger of a life-ending, terminal event. All investigations and therapy had been to no avail. He and his wife had come to Johns Hopkins as a last-ditch effort, hoping for some kind of a miracle. Hopkins was a place where miracles were not uncommon.

The General's wife was asking me about her husband, as we stood outside the door to his room. A muffled scream and strangled cry was clearly heard despite the closed door. We rushed into the room only to find the General in convulsions, struggling to breathe, his airway totally obstructed, his face a darkened mask of blue-purple, his neck extended backward in trismus. (a rigid, unrelenting muscular spasm). His wife had run into the room right behind me and now stood at the foot of the bed, sobbing and crying out in anguish.

My first thoughts were, *"I've got to get his airway open immediately. Keep concentrated. Block out everything else."*

Suddenly, it was as if the General and I were alone in the room, very much like the feeling had been in college playing basketball before thousands of screaming fans. A quick struggle to open his spastic mouth and clenched teeth, using a handy wooden tongue blade, proved fruitless. The intense pressure of his closed teeth and spastic muscles of his mouth broke the stick into pieces. Time is running, got to hurry, what am I going to do? There were no other regular tools available.

Frantically searching for ideas, I spied an old fashioned, metal fly swatter with the doubled-loop wire handle lying upon the window ledge beside the bed. Better to risk germs than be dead. That handle, I thought, ought to be strong enough to do the job. His wife was screaming behind me. Improvising, I snatched the fly swatter off the shelf. Using the handle, I succeeded in prying the mouth open and depressing the tongue forward. As I leveraged the airway open, I was greeted with a violent gush of air erupting into my face, a grateful occasion for both of us. Crude, I know, but it worked.

I thought, *Whew, what a relief! That was a near thing. Not bad work for a young doc just three months out of med school, son.* I began to relax, pleasantly satisfied with my results.

Too quickly accepting the laurels of victory naturally invites disaster. At that precise moment calamity struck. The General's heart arrested, stopped completely, and his breathing ceased. Any hope he had to survive now rested in my untried, solitary hands.

The idea of Cardiopulmonary Resuscitation (CPR) for cardiac arrest had just been pioneered at Hopkins, and had been explained to the interns and residents. A first trial of cases had already recovered by the new technique of external cardiac massage and mouth-to-mouth respiration.

Get with it, use the new CPR maneuvers. I slammed his sternum (breastbone) with my fist. Using my hands, I began to crash my full weight down upon his chest center in a rhythmic cycle every second, counting one-thousand-for each second of time elapsed. Each forceful effort was an attempt to compress the heart and force a pulsation of blood out into the arteries, careless as to whether any rib might be broken, intent only to save him, following the techniques of our instructions.

Mouth to mouth resuscitation, by blowing deep breaths of fresh air into his mouth, was the only means by which I was able to offer him sorely needed oxygen. A hasty check revealed no heart beat. I resumed my efforts. *Am I running out of time?* I was worrying that the time limit to prevent permanent brain damage was approaching. An eternity of time seemed to pass, but in reality had been only a minute or two.

Another listening moment, using the stethoscope around my neck. *Nothing yet.*

The accelerated sounds of his wife moaning and crying loudly in the background barely penetrated my concentration. She did not distract me from the critical matter at hand. I might have been the picture of coolness and disinterest to an observer, but my emotions were running at least as high as hers at that moment. My only thoughts at that time were, *Can I get his heart started and save him? Am I compressing his heart adequately? Am I not? Am I breathing enough for him? Is it going to be too late if the heart does start? Can I save the General? We need your help, Lord.*

A few more disappointments, then suddenly, as if in answer to my plea, the General's heart started back up, at first irregularly, but swiftly becoming a regular rhythm. "*Thank you, Lord,*" I prayed silently. The General began to breathe regularly again, his normal color returned, just as help began to arrive and pour into the room. Oxygen and IV's were started, EKG was done and other medications were administered. The General had survived a precarious situation, but his future was still very much in doubt.

Subsequently, it was determined the malignant hypertension of the General was caused by one severely diseased kidney, secreting a chemical called renin into his blood stream. This chemical causes blood pressure to rise ever higher, leading to blindness, convulsions and death in a fairly short period of time. The official medical term is Unilateral Renal Disease. Removing the diseased kidney would remove the source of the renin. After the surgery was performed, the General's blood pressure returned to normal, his complete vision returned, and he and his wife happily returned to Peru to a full and normal life. I never expected to hear from them again.

As I read and re-read their thoughtful and sincere document, a wonderful feeling crept over me, a feeling hard to describe, but easy to understand. My battery was recharged, like I was the Wright Brothers and had just lifted off successfully, maybe like the feeling of the disciples when Jesus arose on the third day, or like I had just hit a home run in Yankee Stadium with the bases loaded.

The timely expression of gratitude by the General and his wife was a catalyst that rekindled and lit a flame of re-enthusiasm in my original belief in the correctness of my life's chosen work. A feeling of dedication and commitment surged through me once again. I decided that I *would* undertake the additional four or five year struggle to become a surgeon. The worthy goal previously set had not yet been reached. I *would* continue, determined to accomplish that task.

More than 7,000 hospital surgery operations, and more than 688,000 patient office visits would follow in what I called my own version of a ministry. CPR became more refined and commonplace with the passage of time. I chose to remain commonplace myself, in a common place where the blue-collar working-man lived, and where I was most needed. I also chose not to worry too much about refinement.

Throughout the many years of my later medical practice, there were many times I felt again the urge to abandon my commitment to the world of medicine and surgery. As surely as one day follows another, each time I reached that low point there would occur some similar event of inspiration to help me stay the true course, just as happened on that fateful Christmas Eve.

The little silver llama always sat within sight upon a nearby shelf, a constant reminder of commitment with its silent encouragement, until one day it disappeared into someone else's hands who must have thought they needed it more than I. Hopefully, it did as much good for the new owner who took it as it had done for me.

❋ ❋ ❋

How strange are the twists and turns that lead us inexorably down the paths of our lives. Among the options we encounter at various crossroads, the pathways we select have profound consequences—some good, some bad, some regretful. I left for college determined to return and be of service by teaching high school history and coaching basketball. My role model up until that time was my high school teacher and coach, Andy Anderson, a kind and gentle man, once the captain of the University of Georgia basketball and baseball teams.

At each new fork in the roadway of life, we have to make new decisions. In my case, I rejected a scholarship to law school, (I dislike squabbling and disputes), considered the ministry but felt unworthy, finally came to the conclusion medicine would be the best service I could administer unto people, my own form of a ministry. I thought I had consciously made these decisions myself. Many years were required before I realized that I had been guided to my eventual destiny. The only explanation I can suggest to explain how a boy without riches could eventually end up where I was, practicing surgery, is that luck or a guiding spirit, a guardian angel, must have been looking over my shoulder the whole time, and had plans for me which I did not fully recognize, whereby I was led to that improbable place where I would be able to perform the most good for the most people in a needy area. I needed those people as much as they needed me.

A TENDER STORY

Her severe pain was immediately apparent as she limped into one of the examining room. Mrs. Jones was quite old with wrinkled face, gnarled arthritic hands, her hair thin and stringy. Her white-haired husband was stooped over, the ravages of a life of hard labor. His bony hands were large and knobby, with a noticeable Parkinson intention tremor. Their clothes were tattered and showed long use, but were clean, as was the pale whiteness of their skin. It was obvious they were very poor, but proud.

"Doc," the old gentleman started, "my little Bessie has suffered with this pain in her foot for four or five months now. We've done gone all over for help, and they ain't done nothing. We done been sent from one doctor to another, all over Atlanta, even out to Lawrenceville, too. All they did wuz take what little money we get from our old age pension, which ain't much, and send us on to another one who did the same."

It was obvious they were desperately poor. Mr. and Mrs. Jones were living as caretakers of a well-known Atlanta dentist's piece of rural farmland, in return for which they were allowed to live in a small shack on the premises, with no plumbing, assisted by their minimal Social Security income. They had no means of transportation except to find an accommodating friend or church member to take them anywhere. For four months they had been referred back and forth by a cornucopia of chiropractors, podiatrists, and at least one physician, whose name was familiar to me, across Atlanta's huge metropolitan area and to small outlying towns in the suburbs, often entailing a round trip of one hundred miles or more, transported by an accommodating friend or church member. They had been charged for multiple X-rays and office visits, numerous lab tests and physical treatments during the course of these travels. Her pain had not abated, only worsened.

About one minute was all that was required to examine her foot and ankle and realize immediately that she obviously had an inflamed tendon and joint, sometimes called tenosynovitis. Any competent physician could have come to the same easy conclusion, and with the same dispatch. Rather than subject these people to more unnecessary X-rays and lab tests, I explained what was likely the cause of her pain, and what needed to be done.

"I believe I can help you get rid of this problem by putting some special medicines into the area of pain with an injection, or shot." The process was explained n detail to them. Both Mr. And Mrs. Jones looked a little dubious about the whole thing, but remained silent. I felt pretty sure they were thinking, "How he could tell so quickly what was wrong with the foot?" and "If a shot would help, why hadn't somebody else already done it?"

"Honey," Mr. Jones said to his wife, "I been thinking it over. I believe you should go on and try it, 'cause ain't nothing else helped up to now." She looked steadily at him and decided to make the decision unanimous, by saying, resignedly, "I reckon so." He reached over and held her hand tenderly, patting it softly, lending his moral support.

A standard mixture of Xylocaine and an anti-inflammatory, long-acting steroid, Depo-Medrol, with just a "touch" of dexamethasone and Celestone Soluspan added, was instilled into the involved area by injection via a very tiny needle.

"Now, please stand up and walk for me," I encouraged immediately afterwards. Reluctantly, she arose slowly, anticipating the same old pain, and took the first step on the affected leg. Her jaw dropped open, totally agape. An incredulous look on her face was swiftly followed by an enormous, grinning look of relief. "It don't hurt no more," she exclaimed breathlessly to her husband. The two of them looked at each other as if in disbelief at the sudden turn of events.

That sequence of events told me all I needed to know. For the first time in months, she had relief, which greatly pleased all three of us. The immediacy of relief from pain was simply the result of the Xylocaine, but this assured me the remainder of the medicines were in the correct site and the steroids would steadily resolve the inflammation. It also confirmed that my diagnosis was correct.

My own happiness at the result was nearly on the same level as hers for having been the instrument of relieving her constant, debilitating pain. It was always so with me. The great joy and satisfaction I experienced in such situations never abated through the four decades of my medical practice.

They continued to stare at me, with a look of amazement. The old gentleman queried, almost in a whisper, "What is this, a miracle?"

"No," I said, "just something almost any doctor could do. I'm mighty pleased you feel better, Mrs. Jones, but it may be very sore later when it wakes up. We know the medicine is in the right place now, and you should get well." I gave them some samples of anti-inflammatory pills to take, as well as instructions to apply an ice pack, if available, when they returned home, and to apply heat beginning the following day.

"Why didn't any of them others that took our money know that?" Mr. Jones wanted to know, and it was a good question, perhaps best left unanswered.

I tactfully dodged that bullet with, "I can't be sure." The answer plainly did not satisfy him, and it was not, I thought, a satisfactory answer, but Mr. Jones decided, after some consideration, to accept it.

"Now, how much do we owe *you*, doctor?"

I replied, "You don't owe me anything." Their meager funds had already been over-burdened by their "round robin" and sundry travels, referred from place to place seeking relief, to no avail.

"What?" The incredible look of surprise resurfaced upon his face again, and kindled another one of those warming moments that always reminded me why I chose to become a doctor in the first place, and made me thankful once again that I had.

"No, I was glad you gave me the opportunity to help. Now, if you can, put some ice on that for a while when it begins to wake up, okay? Please let me check it in about a week."

His mouth remained agape. She stood, walked about freely, came and hugged my neck, looked into my eyes and said, "Thank you, doctor." I knew she meant it. Recovering, her husband continued to thank me all the way to the door. I watched through the window as they continued to walk away from our office building, excitedly talking and gesturing to each other, still grinning as they turned the corner, out of my sight.

One week later, I noticed a frayed, much-used small brown paper bag upon the front desk of the receptionist. It was twisted and closed at the top, the paper showing the ravages of its past journeys by a geographic network of fine wrinkling. My receptionist said the man who brought it was waiting to see me, and that it was Mr. Jones.

Mr. Jones stepped into the hallway, offered his hand, which I took, and informed me, "The wife is outside in a church friend's pickup truck. She is fine now, so she didn't want to bother you again, but we want you to know we are mighty grateful. The Good Lord knows, Doc, that we ain't got much, but I brought you a bag of these here scuppernong grapes I picked just for you, and I hope you like 'em. It ain't much, but it's all we got."

The scuppernong grape, a variety of the muscadine grape, is sweet and tasty with a faint suggestion of an acidic tang. It can be eaten directly, made into preserves or jellies, and is used to make wine. The scuppernong grape is a revered and enjoyed tradition in the South.

Mr. Jones picked up the bag and tentatively extended it to me. My eyes watered up as I accepted his tendered gift, the best he could offer. "I love scuppernongs, Mr. Jones, and I thank you for going to so much trouble to bring them. Our whole office staff will enjoy them. Each time we take a grape, it will remind us to be thankful to you for bringing them."

The brown paper bag showed signs of much previous use and re-use, wrinkled and sagging, but holding intact its contents, twisted round and round near the top to make the bag closed. It was placed atop the desk of the receptionist.

After searching our eyes, Mr. Jones seemed to sense that we were sincerely appreciative. Pleased that we liked his gift, he said, happily, "I'll tell the little wife, she will be glad."

One last handshaking, and Mr. Jones left the hallway and headed for the front door of the office. At the exit doorway he turned and shyly smiled, slightly nodding his head twice, as he saw me looking. His silent lips mouthed the words, "Thank you," once more and he left.

Through the back office window I watched as Mr. Jones walked slowly toward an old rusted Ford pickup truck, beside which Mrs. Jones was standing. A man in faded blue overalls got out of the driver's seat as Mr. Jones approached. Mr. Jones was speaking to the two of them, his hands forming the shape of the brown bag. It was plain to see by her expression that Mrs. Jones was happy that their scuppernongs were joyfully received.

The old gentleman put his arms around his darling wife, and hugged her to him. She hugged him back in a brief embrace. Mr. Jones kissed her forehead with a short peck, and protecting her every movement by holding her elbow, he gently helped her around the truck to the passenger side, and into her seat. They may have been poor in material things of life, but they shared together a richness of love that many would envy. I noticed with satisfaction that she was not limping as she walked. The truck headed out of the parking lot, and I headed back down the hallway to help the next patient.

At lunch with our staff later that day, we gathered about the bag to enjoy a few of the scuppernong grapes. I unwound the twisted top, and placed my hand inside to retrieve the first grapes. To my immediate and painful surprise, I was stung on the finger by a yellow jacket bee. The yellow jacket had probably slipped into the bag while Mr. and Mrs. Jones were turned away, picking more grapes. I am confident it was not any form of an intentional incident or message.

After the surprise and the laughter settled down, I turned to the rest of the office staff and said, "The moral of this story is that the practice of medicine while attempting to help our fellow man is a roller-coaster of wonderful moments of joy and satisfaction—but not without its occasional sting."

THE GREEN DOOR OF RACISM

"You ain't gonna live long, doc. Don't you understand?"

The three men sat menacingly close around me in my medical office. They had cornered me there. It was the end of the day. Every one else had gone. The heavy-set one with the beer belly and the cigar stub slowly moving in his mouth had just spoken. The pock-faced man cleaning his nails with the point of a knife blade just stared at me, with a look of calculated intimidation.

The third, red-faced man looked nervous, rhythmically tilting back and forth his upper body slowly, changing positions every few minutes, a stain at the corner of his mouth marking the site of a small escape of his chewing tobacco, which he swapped from side to side in his mouth to the same rhythm. Occasionally, he pulled a plastic cup having a Coca-Cola logo upon it to his mouth, into which he would spit.

"I have every expectation of living quite a while," I replied, while trying to mask my uneasiness at being isolated in my office, surrounded, and threatened.

He continued, "You better think it over real careful-like, doc." He leaned close enough for his bad breath to be noticeable.

The man with the knife added, "Bad accidents happen to people all the time, you know." He stared at me, unblinking, to be sure I understood his point.

The heavy-set man said, "Open that door back like it was before, put that sign back up, and don't make no more waves around here." Leaning close into my face, he added, pronouncing each word slowly for emphasis, "Or else, you're asking for it, and you'll get it. We don't want no changes around here, stirring up trouble. You got the message? You cain't say you ain't been warned."

I remained silent. Apparently satisfied, and feeling successful with their threats, the three looked at each other, nodded agreement, arose and left my office by the door at the rear.

I knew why they had come, I had expected something like this. A couple of days earlier, at lunchtime, the carefully planned, long-awaited time had finally arrived. I had walked into the breezeway between my office and the office of the dentist across the way in our small, two-office professional building. I carried a hammer, very long, large diameter nails, a paint brush, and a bucket of green paint. The large nails were hammered through the edges of the door, firmly fixing it into place in the doorframe. Once satisfied the door was properly closed in this first step toward oblivion as a passageway, I then took the paint brush and painted the entire door green, covering over the lettering on the door which proclaimed the entrance to be the "COLORED ENTRANCE."

The news had spread rapidly. The three men did not confirm their status, but implied they were representative members from the Ku Klux Klan. If I did not comply and return the clinic to a segregated status, their threats were meant to be followed by actions that would be physical, severe, and final.

It was 1966. As a 33 year-old physician just starting his practice, I settled into Jonesboro, Georgia, a sleepy, county-seat village a few miles south of Atlanta. At that time the population was comprised mostly of "blue collar" working class people, about 97% white, with 3% non-white, with a county-wide population of only about 80,000, soon to grow to several hundred thousand and become part of Metropolitan Atlanta. Hospital facilities at that time, however, were in Atlanta. Other physicians who had formerly tried to practice there warned me to expect my patients not to pay their medical bills. They said it was the "tradition" in Jonesboro and Clayton County.

The cliques in control of the town, both politically and socially, were the same as in many small towns in the South, having grasped control either by heritage, lineage or by having moderate success in small businesses such as a grocery store, hardware store, vegetation nursery, insurance agency, gas station, upholstery shop, or working for the county at the courthouse.

I was to discover that a number of those in control of local or county affairs had less than a high school education, held strong convictions, and were determined that no changes occur. The local attitude about most things was deeply ingrained and had not changed much from generation to generation for more than a century. Segregation remained as an established protocol.

Chief claims to fame in Jonesboro in those days lay in two areas. First and foremost, Margaret Mitchell in her fictional book, "Gone With The Wind," mentioned Jonesboro as the site of Scarlet O'Hara's plantation, "Tara." In Jonesboro, people hold this is to be very important and still a source of pride, as though it were not fiction, but real. Likely sites of Tara are pointed out. Children are named Tara. Streets are named Rhett Butler and Scarlett O'Hara. Claims are made that Margaret Mitchell used a diary of a Maggie Fitzgerald to write her saga, and gave out to the local gentry recipes from it, including barbecue sauces used locally.

Held in awe almost to the same level is the fact that during the Civil War, Jonesboro was involved in a two day battle associated with the cutting off of supplies to besieged Atlanta. My great grandfather fought for the Confederacy there. The railroad that delivered supplies was interrupted just north of Jonesboro at an intersection called Rough and Ready, today known as Mountain View, Georgia.

The headstone markers in the Confederate Cemetery cover a large mass burial grave for soldiers of both sides, blue and gray. Three thousand poorly armed Confederate soldiers were reportedly wounded or killed in the first thirty minutes of the battle on the west side of Jonesboro. Relics are still found today. Following the battle, the railroad station and most of the housing in Jonesboro were destroyed. Two large Georgian homes with columns survived, being used as hospitals for the wounded and dying.

The Ku Klux Klan was a power in the county, said to be the central headquarters in the KKK for the entire state. Racial segregation was still present throughout the entire local region, as well as most of the South.

My office was in a small office building built by the dentist, from whom I was leasing my space. He said he had used architectural plans devised by Sears and Roebuck as economical, functional, quite popular and widely used throughout parts of the country at the time. Each of the two offices was a mirror image of the other. My side of the office building included a rather large reception area with seating for twenty-six, and an entrance door labeled "For Whites Only."

The plans, almost as an after thought, had a separate entry marked "For Colored People," which opened into a tiny, dimly-lit room that had one short bench filling the space along one wall and capable of holding only three to four people at any one time. The opposite wall had a cut-out opening into the receptionist office, which was located between the two reception rooms. The remaining wall contained a door giving access to a very small, combined utility room-bathroom in the hallway for use by people using the small "waiting" room.

I was born a son of the South, but my training and experience in Indiana, Kentucky, Maryland, San Francisco, New Orleans, Washington, D.C. as well as the U.S. Army had exposed me to a wide experience over much of the United States, with new perspectives. My horizons had broadened.

I told Dr. Walt Spivey, the dentist who owned the building, "Walt, this reception arrangement disturbs me greatly. Something has *got* to be done about it. When I see certain patients, Walt, I am embarrassed for them and feel ashamed of myself." For examples, I named to him a few members of the black community who were pastors, teachers, successful businessmen, farmers, and other well-respected individuals, with or without advanced educations.

He replied, "Yeah I know. I don't know what to do. This is a big KKK county. It's always been this way, Ernie. It needs changing though, I agree." He offered no suggestions, however.

One day I got my courage up enough to broach the subject with a remarkable black lady I had come to know as a patient who had obviously suffered the indignity of that small waiting room and never complained. Mrs. Sharpe was highly educated, and married to Reverend Harold Sharpe. They were to become my main collaborators in a scheme to change things.

"Mrs. Sharpe, I know I am late in this, but I want you to know how I feel about something that has been troubling me."

With her usual demeanor of pleasantness, she smiled and asked, "What is that, Doctor?"

"That small waiting room, and it's not because it is small. It's what goes with it."

She understood immediately, but wisely waited to see what it was that I was about to say.

"I want to do something about it, Mrs. Sharpe. It really bothers me, especially when I see people like you or your husband. Please understand me, that sign has to go and that room needs closing—to *everybody*, not just you."

"Yes, it does," she replied calmly. "Are you planning to do it?"

That question finally triggered a germ of an idea into action. "I could use your help. We would need to move slowly and try to gradually develop the idea, rather than precipitate a violent storm reaction, don't you think?"

She did not reply, just looked steadily at me, probably suspecting the worst, and disappointment.

I continued, "Maybe, try to get the idea across by actions, or activities, that awaken people to the situation more practically. You are a teacher, let's try to educate by example. You and Reverend Sharpe can help on your end and I will on mine. Don't give up on me. Be patient for a time. We shall get it done."

She agreed, but I thought to myself, *"She probably thinks this is all horsefeathers, lip service, or a lot of bull and nothing will change."*

Nevertheless, I soon was joined by the addition of other conspirators. We had both white and black people helping, by entering alone, or sometimes together, and remaining seated in the larger "white" reception area, talking calmly together until called by the nurse. We had young black males volunteer to enter the so-called "white" waiting area and create a loud, angry scene about being ordered to the "black" waiting room, refusing to go. The idea was that this was for others in the waiting room to hear, think about, and talk about. Hopefully, this was a process of education to these observers. We made a point of showing respect to each and all in equal fashion. Sure, I had complaints, but they were surprisingly, and happily, very few.

Finally, for no particular reason, I chose the day. It was as good a day as any. I bought my supplies at the hardware store. At lunchtime, while others were lunching, I nailed that infamous green door shut, and painted over the "For Colored People" sign. Later that day, arrangements were made by telephone to have the door permanently sealed. Huge bolts and inner braces were used. The door was never again opened. The tiny room was converted for office administration purposes. Only the large reception area remained, to be shared by all.

It was a form of culture shock to the entire area, more severe to some than to others. Until that time, such a thing had not occurred anywhere in the region. Fortunately, it was taken in stride, quietly approved, and accepted by the vast majority of the populace.

My threatening visitors, presumably from the Ku Klux Klan, had departed, confident in the success of their mission. They had cowered the new doc. They did not know that I had considered what they had said, and had resolved to stay the course.

Only a few months earlier I had been discharged from the U.S. Army, after my experiences in an overseas combat area. I was quite familiar with firearms, and a qualified expert with the .45 caliber automatic pistol, for example. For the next few months, my patients would probably have been shocked had they known underneath my starched laboratory coat lay a hidden shoulder holster with a .45 caliber pistol, loaded and ready. Above my ankle rested a holster with a .38 caliber pistol, also loaded. To a few well-selected sources I let it be known I was well-armed. Being armed proved to be a wise precaution.

On the way home from the hospital quite late one night, a large pickup truck, containing men in the cab and several men in the open bed at the back of the truck, pulled alongside me and forced my car off the road, cutting into my car at an angle. I was cutoff and blocked at the roadside, as the men began jumping out of the truck, shouting as they ran toward my little MGB convertible with the top down.

Instinctively, I reached for my .45 caliber pistol in the shoulder holster, but came up empty. However, I recalled it was under the seat and quickly had it in my hand. I could have easily fired into several of the rushing crowd, but there were too many. Instead, I slammed the MGB roadster into reverse, scratched off backwards, while whipping the car around in a circle to head in the opposite direction.

Looking back in the mirror, I saw they could never get everyone loaded, turn that big truck around, and catch up to me. I took several circuitous routes homeward. I'll never know exactly to what end that night's threat was intended, but the circumstances indicated it was my three visitors and people of their ilk. It was the only incident of significance to ever interrupt an otherwise quiet, peaceful transition in our community.

Totally unrelated to my own initiative, but soon to follow, like a house of cards falling, it was amazing how fast all doors marked "For Colored People" were no longer to be seen. It should have been much earlier. Many of the younger generation now have come to believe it has always been what they see today, and maybe that is a good thing. Let the past sleep, and get on with the living.

Mrs. Sharpe and I have remained close and loyal friends. She is now a highly placed official in the State of Georgia Education Department. Regrettably, my friend Reverend Harold Sharpe passed away. Many years later, a middle-aged black man walked into my office, having just moved from California. He reminded me he had been one of the young conspirators who made loud, disruptive scenes in the "white" reception area.

We had some good laughs together. We talked about those old days, how we had worked together to bring down the "For Colored People" sign, our own symbolic wall of Jericho. We were both glad that the changes can now be taken for granted by future generations.

There have always been some people who are racists. There always *will* be some people who are racists. Sadly, most of the racists I have encountered the last number of years are not white people, but are the very ones who lived under, and decried, racism earlier, and now are racists themselves.

"Colored People" they were called in earlier days in the South. Later they came to prefer to be called black people, or Afro-Americans. Lately, some of them are now preferring to be spoken of as "People of Color," which makes it seem this presently chosen form of nomenclature has gone full circle back to where it was earlier, a curious cycle. At the same time the role of racists have been largely reversed.

My family name is a Scot name. My family lineage dates back in America to the Revolutionary War era. It would be silly if I insisted upon myself being called a Scot-American, or Anglo-American. I am proud of my Scot and English heritage, as well as my Southern heritage, but I prefer to be called simply an American. After all, that is what we are, each and every one of us. The sooner that is realized and accepted by all of the citizenry, the better chance we have to enjoy opportunities of peace, harmony and equality.

Andrew Young, former Mayor of Atlanta and the United Nations Representative has a dentist brother, Walter Young, a successful dentist and investor, with whom I had the privilege of sharing an evening visiting the home of two brothers, Italian Counts. We were sitting around the kitchen table, talking friendly about this and that. During the discussion of topical interests, the subject of racism happened to surface, and Walt became animated, using the word racist a number of times to describe certain people.

"Walter," I interjected, politely, "I notice you are using the word *racist* a great deal. I want to tell you something about how I feel on the subject."

He looked and me and said, "What?"

Trying to draw this nice man toward some of my insight, I ventured, "I am a racist, Walter." It had the effect I desired. There was a surprised silence at the table. The two Italian Counts sat among the group and, upon my words, glanced nervously at each other. Walter's mouth gaped a little, as he stared at me intently, probing. I hoped my planned nefarious approach was going to prove successful. I knew it would going to be like balancing while walking on a high wire circus act, but felt the risk was worth the effort.

"Yes, Walter, I am a racist." Then I added, "You see, Walt, personally I am for the *whole, entire* human race, not just any *one* segmental race of any particular kind. I guess that would qualify me as a racist, wouldn't it, in favor of *all* of the human race." That was about as far as I felt I could go, trying to make my point. I was not sure I got my message across, but I hoped so.

He continued to stare at me for a bit, pondering the idea, and me, but said not one word. He probably thought *me* to be a simpleton, but I don't believe *he* got it, because he slowly turned and resumed his rhetoric. Our roundtable conversation eventually moved on to various other topics.

THE HOCKEY STICK

The insistent ringing of the bedside telephone successfully penetrated the gray matter of my fogged sleeping brain, and won the battle. A bit of fumbling with the coiled line yielded the phone, into which I struggled to emit a squeaky, but civil, and eventual, "Hello."

"Doc, this is Detective Martin."

"What time is it?"

"Just past three."

A faint groan escaped my lips. I remembered Detective Martin from our work together previously on several cases in which I had been called. He was a brown-haired, pleasant man about thirty years old, beginning to show an early expansion of his belt line, always dressed in the same dark blue suit, never seemed to tire, always as fresh as an early morning dew, a ready cup of coffee in his hand, or nearby. Peculiar, I just realized his first name was still unknown to me.

"I bet I know, another rape case, right?" Already into the seventh years of examining every suspected case of rape, usually in the wee hours of the night, had played heck with my sleep schedule, but it was my duty as the police surgeon and official Clayton County Physician. On each occasion, I rued the day I had volunteered.

"Not this time. Doc, do you know anything about a letter talking about a hockey stick from the Atlanta Flames, or something like that?"

His words caught me off guard. "Why, yeah. I just dictated such a letter myself yesterday afternoon, to the Atlanta Flames. It was about a hockey stick." Surely, the Atlanta Flames were not checking on the credibility of my request at three in the morning. Maybe, somehow, the letter had been lost in the mailing and had been found. That seemed unlikely.

"Well, doc, a little while ago we collared a car speeding northbound on I-75 at ninety-five miles an hour in the southbound lane, meeting traffic head-on. The officer in the chase car saw objects flying out the windows of the fleeing car. Two men and a woman in the vehicle were arrested, and we have them here at the county jail."

Puzzled, I asked, "What has that got to do with the hockey stick?"

"I'm coming to that. We went back and found several of the items that were thrown out. They were vials of medicines for injection. One is named T-a-l-w-i-n. Another one is h-y-d-o-x-y-z-i-n-e. We found three others, and some more stuff, too."

What this had to do with the letter about hockey sticks, I could not imagine. It seemed to be a routine arrest of drunks, or druggies, with erratic driving habits, except the weird presence of the relatively harmless medicines Martin named which mystified me.

A stirring in the bed beside me prompted, "Hold on a minute, Martin. My wife is waking up. I'll go to the kitchen, be there in a jiffy." Poor girl, she doesn't need to lose her beauty sleep, too. I was resigned to my own fate.

Reaching the kitchen, I headed for an old middle-of-the-night friend, the stainless steel coffeepot sitting stoically next to the telephone, ever ready to perk me up. The pot was handy in this convenient spot, always loaded and ready to serve night or day. I pushed the on switch. The conversation thus far was giving every indication I would be sleepless the rest of the night. Why did it seem to be always in the wee hours of the night that this kind of duty called?

"The vials of medicine you mentioned, Martin, are not narcotics, but I'll be glad to look the lot over for you in the morning." Maybe a little more sleep was in the offing, after all. It was worth a try.

"Doc, we'd like you to come down to the station now, while we are holding the two men and the woman. You can look over the vials for us, so we'll know what we have to work with here."

"Why did you ask about the Atlanta Flames and the hockey stick?"

"Well doc, the arresting officer was really on the ball. He noticed the edge of something sticking out from underneath the passenger seat. He pulled it out and it was a small tape recorder. When he pushed the play button, a man's voice was talking about a letter to the Atlanta Flames about a hockey stick. A girl was mentioned, too."

His words startled me. Recovering my surprise and composure, I replied, "Good lord, Martin. That sounds like a letter I dictated to the Atlanta Flames yesterday afternoon." I felt obliged to explain. "One of my patients, a girl named Betsy, really has me worried. She is a lonely, extremely depressed, teen-age girl. Betsy has lived on crutches all her life, crippled since birth. Her family mostly ignores her, favoring her healthy sisters. Like a lot of other young girls in Atlanta, Betsy feels strongly attracted to young Jacque Richard of the Atlanta Flames. Because I'm worried about her mental condition, I requested a hockey stick autographed by Richard to surprise her, to lift her spirits, hopefully. How in the world did it get there? "

"That's what we wondered, too." I didn't like the tone of his statement. Is Martin implying something here, about a relationship between the culprits and me, or am I over-reading his statement?

"Will you come down to the station and help us sort it out?" It was nice he asked instead of telling me.

"Sure." What else could I say? "I'll be right down." Expedience can be the mother of laziness, but was vice-versa, in this case, encouraging me to hustle into pants pulled on hastily to cover pajamas. A coat was grabbed, and I was on my way, still wearing bedroom slippers.

My curiosity was tweaked. A need to know was beginning to ferment within me, threatening to overflow like a kettle of boiling water. How did my tape get in their possession? Wait a minute, the tape recorder was probably mine also. Oh, no, not *another* break-in at my clinic.

Burglars had previously entered the office by shattering the entire heavy-glass front door on a Christmas Eve, another time by removing the entire back window frame and setting it upon the ground, also by breaking in through front, side or rear doors on numerous occasions, and once by entering through a skylight in the roof. The thieves made away with all of the office machines and equipment one dark night. Another musically inclined thief stole a treasured classical guitar, which I kept at the office for quiet moments of relaxation. All the other times, it had been addicts looking for possible hard drugs, unaware that no legitimate doctor possesses such things. The damage and mess created in our clinic, however, was always disheartening and disruptive, frustrating enough to make a Baptist preacher get angry and consider taking up cussing, maybe even drinking, or even worse, forget to mention tithing in Sunday's sermon.

At the police station, Martin was sitting at his desk, holding the inevitable cup of coffee, just finishing a sip as I entered. His desk was beneath a darkened window along one wall of a huge room containing fifteen or twenty desks, and people surprisingly busy for this early hour. Crime and domestic violence were apparently having a jubilant local revival tonight. People were working at most of the desks, interviewing people, completing forms, booking people, talking on phones, as other people were entering and leaving the area. A few pale men in prison attire, trustees, moved about the room. One prisoner, in handcuffs. was slowly walking in my general direction, accompanied by an officer.

"Hey, doc. Thanks for coming. We'll take your statement about the vials right here." I plopped down into a creaky, straight-backed wooden chair beside Martin's desk. He handed five vials to me for inspection.

"Let's see." I studied each of the vials carefully. "This one is Talwin, a synthetic non-narcotic pain reliever. The others are hydroxyzine, also a non-narcotic used for itching, nausea or anxiety, this one is sterile distilled water for mixing medicines, the next is Decadron, a steroid anti-inflammatory, and the last is methylene blue, a dye used in the laboratory for testing." The dye caused me to chuckle at what must have been their keen disappointment when they realized they had stolen a vial of useless dye.

"These little colored paper sticks were scattered in their car, doc. What are they?"

I laughed out loud. "Those are dip sticks for testing urine for sugar, albumin and several other things. Yep, I was now sure my office had been sacked again. "What about the recorder and the dictated letter, Martin?"

Martin took another sip of his coffee. I noticed he was wearing his same blue coat. The incongruity of his scuffed brown shoes caught my eye. Although the room temperature was a little cool, it occurred to me I had never seen him without the coat—rain or shine, hot or cold. When he raised the cup again, a class ring from some school or police academy was visible on his left ring finger. I had never noticed it previously. He must not be married, which explained why he worked the night shift so often.

"It's right here." He reached into a large drawer and extracted a small recorder, setting it on the desk in front of me. Residual fine powder in the various grooves and crevices indicated fingerprint testing had been done. I was able to immediately recognize it was my office recorder.

"Yep, that's my recorder, for dictating letters. It has my social security number on the side." I pushed the rewind button, then play, and the soft southern accent of my own voice greeted me, pleading for help to pull a deeply depressed, crippled teenage girl out of the doldrums by the simple expedient of an autographed hockey stick from her idolized hockey player.

Martin was busy writing down all I was saying, but he looked up and asked me point blank, "Do you recognize anyone in this room other than the officers and clerks you know from your official duties as police surgeon and County Physician?" Did I just imagine Martin seemed to tense up, as though in anticipation, as he leaned forward expectantly?

His nervous inquiry caused me to glance around the room. A couple of cases were being booked, several people were apparently visiting for their own unknown reasons, a man was resting his head on a desk. Three prisoners in jail garb were moving about the room in a haphazard manner, and the prisoner in handcuffs was walking slowly along the aisle adjacent to the desk where we sat, the officer tagging along with him.

"No, I don't recognize any one."

"How about that one? He nodded specifically at the man in handcuffs walking back and forth slowly in the adjacent aisle. The man appeared to be in his thirties, with sandy-grayish curly hair, about five feet ten inches tall, one hundred-sixty pounds, a face pock marred and scarred. Despite being a prisoner in handcuffs, he was walking along casually with the officer, his attitude one of complete unconcern, as if he was quite at home in a jail.

"Nope, never saw him or any of the others before."

Martin continued to stare, then visibly relaxed and returned to his writing. When he felt everything was down on paper to his satisfaction, he turned and said, "Thanks, doc, that's all. Will you come by and sign this document for me in the morning, when we have it completed?"

"Sure, I'm going back home to catch a few winks. Well, good night."

About seven o'clock the following morning I stopped a little early while on the way to my office, ready to sign the papers. Martin was still there, trying to finish up. I asked, "What have you learned from the three prisoners?"

"The two men turned out to be brothers. The woman and the younger brother are still in jail. The other brother was the one you saw in handcuffs last night. He managed to make bond and has already left jail."

The realization came slowly. He was referring to the prisoner in handcuffs who had been paraded before me, surreptitiously and systematically, to see if either of us might show some signal of recognition of the other. The idea they might have suspected me of collusion awakened my mental faculties and infuriated me. I seethed inside at the implications, but managed to keep the hurt hidden.

I asked, incredulously, "You guys let him *go*?"

"He made bond, we had no choice. The girl and the younger brother could not make bond and are still in jail."

"When you checked my office, what did you find? What can I expect to find when I get there shortly?"

"Uh, doc, we didn't check your office," as an after thought, "yet." He bit his lip, and added, "You see, we are County Police and your office is not in our jurisdiction. The Jonesboro Police will have to do that. A flitting, transient nervous tic flashed about his left eye orbit. Items scattered upon the top of his desk suddenly needed shuffling and rearranging. He avoided facing me. I took that to mean he was personally ashamed of his earlier subterfuge, however, I knew it was part of his job to be suspicious.

I understood. The chronic sequel of dealing with criminals, cheats, con men, liars, drug addicts, and the dredges of society leads law enforcers to become hardened, and to expect the worst of people and to be overly suspicious of everyone. I had just been included in their ring of suspicions, making sure that I was not involved with the threesome in some way. Being included in their suspicions should not have surprised me, but it did. It is not a comfortable position in which to find one's self, especially when innocent.

At my office I found the entry had been made through the back door by prying open the door frame from the lock, shattering the woodwork. A gentle push was all that was required now to open the door easily. Fortunately, the marauding thieves did not take the office typewriters, copying machine, EKG or other equipment this time. However, the laboratory chemicals and vials were scattered about the floor of the lab and into the hallways, leaving a path of destruction as though a latter-day Sherman had marched through my little medical world in Georgia. They obviously thought the tape recorder would be useful to them, not dreaming it would be the instrument to betray them.

Ivy Sholar, my friend and patient, was a silver-haired and jolly man with a sharp tongue, a quick wit and the owner of the local pawn shop. He also was Chief of the three-man Jonesboro Police Force. He arrived at nine o'clock to dust for fingerprints. The crime was in his jurisdiction. Chief Sholar examined throughout the office and the entry site, where the thief had entered by removing the skylight and dropping into an examining room. I expected little in the way of results. I got what I expected. Sholar tried, but only disarray and destruction were found.

"Chief, who was the officer who responded to the burglar alarm last night?"

A sly smile and raised eyebrows slowly emerged, like a butterfly easing itself out of its cocoon. "Fairly Jackson. He said he drove around the clinic and didn't see anything suspicious." Sholar could not resist repeating, with a chuckle, "That's what he *said*."

I knew Fairly Jackson very well, a pleasant black man, well-liked by all, active in community affairs, a patient of mine, and about to run for public office. I also knew Fairly Jackson was accustomed to nightly sleeping in his patrol car while parked out of sight behind my clinic, a necessity since he also worked a second job in the daytime for the County Police, as he confessed to me when I found him there one night. It became our little shared secret. He was therefore quite familiar with the facility.

In spite of his familiarity with the premises, Jackson was oblivious to the odd arrangement of a stack of exterior benches piled all the way up to the roof as he made his circle in the patrol car. He also missed the burglar, who had returned to the roof after setting off the electronic alarm, and was standing in the open upon the darkened roof. In the thief's rush to escape, he had left his gray hooded sweatshirt behind in the examining room. Chief Sholar examined the sweaty fabric, smelled it, and decided by his experience in such matters that the burglar had to have been a white man. (He was correct, actually.) Mack Sennett could have filmed the entire proceedings with his Keystone Kops. Incredibly, but not surprisingly, no prints were found.

At midday I went to the jail to examine officially the new admissions, a duty I had assumed besides my private practice. Among the new detainees was the female thief of the trio who burgled my office. She looked older and more worn than her 20 years of age, with stringy dyed blonde hair, a mousy face, receding chin, slightly snaggle-toothed, and dirty fingernails. She quietly answered my medical questions as a police matron stood beside us. Among the men examined, I was unsure which might be the young brother, but I noticed the attending officer trying to unobtrusively observe any recognition signals between any of the prisoners and me.

Detective Martin walked in just as I was about to leave. The absence of a coffee cup in his hand was striking, a first. "Doc, we just found out the older brother we let out on bond was wanted in DeKalb County for skipping bail, on a bond of twenty-eight thousand dollars."

"Good grief, you let him go without finding that out? Why wasn't he held until you could check him out today?"

"He knew he was a wanted man, doc. That's why he was so quick to make bond here and get away before morning, but he'll be back for trial."

"Don't count on it. He didn't come back to DeKalb for trial. What makes you so sure he will here?"

He had no answer for that, except to say, "Well, we'll see. C'mon, let's get a cup of coffee." Some things never change.

About two to three months later, the trial was held. The only defendant to show up was the girl, who appeared in court with a high-necked black dress, topped with white lace at the neck, looking innocent as a lamb, prim and proper like a Quaker on the way to church meeting. With her subdued demeanor and angelic presentation, she was the mirror image of Olivia DeHavilland as Melanie in "Gone With the Wind." It must have helped. Although being found guilty, she was released immediately on probation. The younger brother had been released on bail by this time. Neither of the two brothers returned for trial. Nothing was ever heard of the trio again.

The letter to the Atlanta Flames was re-written. Through the back window of my office, about two weeks later, I saw Betsy laboring on her crutches toward the clinic. In addition to the crutches, she was managing somehow to clutch a hockey stick in her hands. I opened the back door and smiled an invitation. Betsy came into my office on her crutches, beaming with the joy. She was holding in her hands a hockey stick of the Atlanta Flames, autographed by their star player, young, handsome Jacque Richard, who seemed to have all of Atlanta's young ladies hearts aflutter, and swooning like Scarlett O'Hara at the mention of Ashley Wilkes name. Only one of that multitude, however, had a genuine, personally autographed Jacque Richard hockey stick, making her very special indeed.

"I wanted you to see this, doctor. You remember us talking about Jacque, when I saw you last visit?" She put her metal crutches against the arms of a chair, handed the stick to me for my inspection, and sat down. The glow of her happiness spread over her face, like the morning sun chasing away darkness, and lighting up the day.

"Vaguely," I lied, pretending innocence. "Wow, Betsy, this is really something, and signed just to you, too. You must be a very special young lady." I returned the stick.

"I guess maybe I am; I have a few friends—like you, Doctor A." She gave me a coy look, to convey she knew exactly what had happened, raised the hockey stick and tipped it to me like the tip of a hat, and said, "Thanks." Betsy was a very bright girl, she had put two and two together and had her suspicions, but Bre'r Fox, he lay low. I neither accepted her insinuation nor rejected it. We chatted a bit, and she left the way she entered, through the private back door. I watched her as she was laboring across the pavement, a determined, smart young lady. Her steps may have been labored, but were filled with a new air of confidence. For some inane reason, a carnival sideshow, or a Vegas Spin-the-Wheel barker came to my mind, "Place your bets, place your bets, folks." Mine is on Betsy. She is on the right track now and will go far, despite her handicap, disproving any notions to the contrary held by her parents, or anyone.

A two-edged sword can cut both ways. The hockey stick had been the equivalent of a three-edged sword: 1) it led to the thieves being captured; 2) Betsy's dangerous depression was lifted; 3) I got my recorder back, but more importantly, I had the immense satisfaction of having helped a young friend in desperate need, at a critical moment.

Betsy graduated from high school, became a successful student at Georgia Tech, and faced life with a new exuberance that began with a simple hockey stick. Sometimes, a little boost by a kind word, a touch, or just knowing someone cares at a critical time can work wonders. The nuisance and expense of a broken skylight, a few vials, and a tape recorder were only a coincidental nothingness besides the joy I felt at the transformation of Betsy, from deep depression into a purposeful, confident young lady with renewed self-esteem, and the direction her life took at this important fork in the roadway of her life. There are many impulsive teen-age suicides in the United States related to depression. Even *one* is too many. I rejoice in gladness for my friend and patient, Betsy.

CHARITY HOSPITAL EMERGENCY ROOM— NEW ORLEANS

The young man stood quietly, nonchalantly chewing on a length of heavy gauge string which dangled from the corner of his mouth, like some people do with a wooden matchstick, even as they talk. I was puzzled as to why he was in this area, amidst a scene of frantic, organized confusion trying to expedite the care of gun-shot wounds, knife-stabbings, broken bones, beatings, car crashes, trauma, nose bleeds, assorted injuries and multiple lacerations, which continued unabated like some combination of a tidal wave, tsunami, and a monsoon, garnished with the disaster of an earthquake, perhaps even an armed banana republic revolution. It was Saturday night in the E. R. at Charity Hospital in New Orleans, Louisiana.

Inquiring, I asked, "Do you have a relative here that we are trying to help?" I had no idea I was about to meet one of my most unforgettable, bizarre cases.

"No, I don't." he replied. He was a black male about twenty-five years of age, 5 feet eleven inches in height, and 170 pounds in weight, wearing a purple shirt and black pants. A sheen of beaded perspiration graced his face.

Presuming him to be the waiting relative of some patient in the ER, I said, "If you are not a relative of a patient," I said, helpfully, "you will have to leave this area."

"No, I don't." A man of few words, apparently the *same* few words.

"And, why not?" He was in no discernible state of agitation that I could detect. He was much calmer than the usual emergency patient that arrived in my domain, the Trauma and Surgical E.R., as opposed to the M. R. (Medical Room), where colds, congestion, sore throats, coughs, chest pain, blood pressure, heart, strokes and other medical type problems were handled; however, New Orleans's multitudinous asthma population, for some strange reason, was treated for *acute* asthma in the surgical emergency area, where on occasion as many as one hundred-fifty to as many as two hundred or more asthmatics might be seen during any night in the E.R.

"I'm here 'cause I got a pain in my th'oat." He was definitely going to stand his ground.

Patients with lacerations were residing on Gurney stretchers up and down the hallways. Surgical suture trays were already resting beside them on the Gurneys, their injuries to be repaired by us as time permitted. In the room and cubicles, the horrendous major cases took priority. All were being attended by the E.R. physician staff, which was comprised of only two interns and me, the surgery resident, accompanied by the nursing staff, the most proficient and dedicated nursing staff I ever encountered, some of whom I rank higher in their professional know-how than many doctors I have known.

With that knowledge gained, I was now quite confident of the situation, and quickly told him, "You will have to go to the Medical Emergency Room for your sore throat. This is the Surgical and Trauma Emergency Room area."

He insisted, "No, I wants to be he'pped right here." He repeated, "*Right* here." He was determined. He knew what he was talking about. I did not.

"We don't treat sore throats here in the E.R." At the same time as I was instructing him, out of an ingrained habit, I pulled my otoscope light out of my pocket to take a quick look at his throat. Maybe, I thought, I could quickly save the over-loaded Medical Emergency room one more patient.

"Open your mouth, I'll take a quick look for you," I said. We live and learn. I was about to be reminded that things are not always what they seem to be, and I would never forget the lesson.

As he opened his mouth, I grasped the string to remove it, and I pulled. He jerked his head forward at me, but the string stayed firmly in his mouth. I pulled again, harder, and his head snapped forward. A series of pulling at the string and letting go of it yielded a curious bobbing backward and jerking forward of his head, looking like a chicken's head and neck when they walk. The string would not come out. Somehow, it was attached.

My curiosity piqued by now, I obtained a laryngoscope and searched deeper into the abyss of his throat, and to my surprise, "what to my wondering eyes should appear" was not a sleigh and eight tiny reindeer, but a fisherman's large fishhook imbedded deep down inside the wall of his throat, attached to the aforementioned line ascending to exit his mouth.

"My gosh, there's a large fish hook stuck in your throat," I exclaimed. My words and the look on my face must have startled him, for he assumed a pained look of disgust on his face as if to say any fool should have known that, but he said not a word in response.

With the aid of a long-handled surgical instrument I was able to extricate the hook and removed the hook and string safely.

I asked, "How in the world did you get a fish hook and line stuck down there, deep in your throat?"

He shuffled from one foot to the other, looked uncomfortable, but remained silent, reluctant to say anything to this simpleton of a doctor who couldn't figure it out without being told.

"Look," I said, "I helped you out of a tough spot and I think you ought to at least tell me how this happened." My curiosity knew no bounds—I was imagining all sorts of possibilities.

He finally yielded, looked around a bit, and seeing no one close at hand, he gave his lips a smacking sound, rolled the tip of his tongue to the side of his mouth, smacked his lips again like he was relishing the ghost of some past savory gastronomic delight, and said, "I was *eatin'* when I got that hard pain in my *th'oat*. I was sucking catfish heads." Well, that floored me, sucking catfish heads certainly had not been in my imaginary list of possibilities.

From a catfish head, he had sucked a hook with its attached line down into his throat and caught himself. It was the most curious, and certainly the biggest, "Catch-Of-The-Day" that I was ever to encounter, human or otherwise.

✻ ✻ ✻

The swarming numbers of emergency patients were like a never-ending tidal wave at Charity Hospital in New Orleans, an historical 3000 bed hospital dating back to the days of the so-called "infamous" Governor Huey Long. Patients were referred from the outlying branch Charity Hospitals throughout the entire state. The New Orleans Emergency Room teems with an unbelievable swarm of a never-ending volume of patients, where the strangest of cases become everyday events.

Ruth, the nurse, called out to me from the other end of the ER hall, "Doctor A, hurry down here, you have to see this."

Ruth was a terrific ER nurse, extremely experienced, wise and efficient. If I were the patient, I would prefer her for the immediate early-reactions supportive care necessary in trauma cases instead of a significant number of doctors I have observed. Ruth knew well the difference between a real emergency and a routine case. There was no urgency in her voice, so I ambled down the hall in the direction of her voice.

She drew back the curtain of the cubicle in which stood, and I entered. My mouth dropped open at what I saw. Even as jaded as one can become in such a hectic ER as Charity, there always kept occurring surprises that would jolt you from time to time. This was one of those times.

The black man standing in front of me was about twenty-five years old. There was dark red blood caking his face, as well as the front of his previously-white tee shirt, along with fresh bleeding dripping from the point of his chin onto the shirt and the floor. He seemed perfectly at peace where he stood, calmly looking me over as though he were the physician and I were the patient. He did not speak.

The incongruent feature of his calm and quiet attitude was a huge meat cleaver, like butchers use, the large blade of which was imbedded vertically in the center of his forehead, the handle hanging down beside his nose, mouth and chin. This particular weapon and placement I had never seen before.

"You have quite a problem," I said to him. "What happened?" Vicarious curiosity must be sated.

"Damn, man, cain't you see?" He was correct. After all, I guess you could say it was rather obvious. It was the gory details of the skirmish I was *really* seeking.

"I can see very clearly the end result. I was just wondering how it came about. Not important, really. Let the police sort it out. Ruth, please get the police officer in here."

At that prospect, he complied quickly, "A friend did it."

A familiar answer, heard so often in the ER. "You need to be more careful picking your friends."

"I know das right," he replied rather wistfully.

"The bleeding seems to be stopped. Send him for tangential X-rays, Ruth, with the cleaver still in place. We'll see if the inner bone plate has been penetrated. Okay?"

"Right."

The X-rays showed the cleaver had not penetrated into the vault containing his brain. Any question as to the *quality* of his brain could not be answered by X-rays. To be found in this position certainly raises the question. With much difficulty the cleaver finally was extracted, the wound was repaired and he waltzed out the door into the night to face further adventures with more of his "friends."

It was not unusual to see a patient walk into the ER with the handle and blade of a butcher knife extending from various points of his body, such as the chest or abdomen, and invariably identify the assailant only as a "friend." I recall one particular case. His dubious explanation is a good example of the evasive answers we received. With a practiced look of genuine sincerity, a butcher knife extruding from the right posterior-lateral of his chest, and said, "All I know is I was jest sitting dere on de curb of de sidewalk, minding my own bizzness when I felt dis pain in my side. When I looked down, I saw dis knife sticking out of me."

"And you have no idea how it got there," I asked, "is that right?"

"Das right. It musta been some friend did it." The code of the street, I presumed. Never squeal or inform. In many such cases I attended, they never did. It was usually a feigned vagueness of recall, substituting the term "friend" or "I dunno." instead of naming the actual culprit. Rare exceptions were severe cases where death or near-death had occurred from such trauma, and a relative or neighbor-witness in moments of extreme emotional grief might reveal the actual name of an assailant.

✺ ✺ ✺

One young Afro-American girl about sixteen years old, presented one late Saturday night with a three inch slicing laceration on the outer side of her left upper arm, seen through the adjoining slashed hole in her blood-soaked long sleeve blouse. As the nurse cut the dangling sleeve away and removed it, at least 60-80 healed scars covering her entire arm came into view. The individual scars varied from one to three inches in length. A look at the opposite arm revealed similar scars all over that arm. No area seemed to be spared, the tracks crisscrossing and covering her arm like some sort of bizarre jigsaw puzzle.

Astounded, I asked, "Why are all these scars on your arms? How did they get there?"

"Same as this one tonight. Me and my girl friend like to have knife fights. We do it all the time. It's fun." An effort was made to dissuade her of this form of recreation, but I had the feeling my breath was being wasted and the effort to change her peculiar persuasion would be ignored.

The pale scars contrasted starkly against the darkness of the skin that remained in the few small areas untouched by healed knife tracks. She had been lucky not to have suffered severed tendons and other serious consequences such as keloids, (over-development of scar tissue, which can sometimes build up to be of enormous size), and infections.

❋ ❋ ❋

Federal Agents brought Carlos Mostellar, reputed Mafia Boss of New Orleans and the surrounding territory, and one of the most powerful men in Louisiana, into the Charity Hospital ER one dark night while I was there. He had been forcibly taken by the feds and had suffered cracked ribs, reportedly caused by resisting their offer to accompany them. After assuring the lungs had not been affected, the ribs were treated by applying a supportive appliance of bandaging. Mr. Mostellar and the Fedederal agents departed. One of the most powerful and feared men in Louisiana had been humbled by being brought to a charity institution for care. Subsequently, it was reported in the newspapers and on TV that Mr. Mostellar had been physically grabbed and illegally, hastily, surreptitiously deported forcibly and immediately to Nicarauga the same night. According to the media, this entire action was carried out, without due process of law, purportedly by the order of Bobby Kennedy, Attorney General of the United States.

❋ ❋ ❋

A thirty-two year-old New Orleans police officer lost control of his car, striking a tree at only 10 mile per hour. He ruptured his lungs and trachea (main breathing tube) and air had leaked out of his chest settling underneath the skin of his chest and neck, swelling him up like a balloon. When his skin was touched, the feel and sound of crackling occurred, like squeezing a bag of popcorn. This is medically referred to as *crepitus*, sometimes as *subcutaneous emphysema*. He had expired before anything could be done for him. It seemed unbelievable that such a slight bump.

should cost someone their life. A sobering lesson about speed for the casual attitude held by today's driver.

❋   ❋   ❋

A twenty-eight year-old Afro-American man was hustled into the ER, unconscious, with the entire left side of his neck laid open by a vicious blow form a hatchet-axe. The wound went all the way into the trachea, larynx area, severing arteries and veins with blood spurting everywhere, his gasping breaths rasping, struggling to suck air into the lungs through the huge open wound and blood flow. He obviously had massive blood loss and was near the point of death. How he made it to the ER still alive, I could not imagine, but he did, and our team jumped into action.

I jammed packing towels into the massive wound laid open and applied pressure, slowing the blood loss, yelling for someone to call the operating room and notify them the nature of the situation and that we were on the way there, while Ruth was getting an IV going, as we simultaneously were hurrying the gurney down the hallway toward the elevator and the seventh floor operating area. The pressured towels were soaked through with blood, however, the blood loss was now welling rather than spurting. Seconds counted, and would make the difference between survival and death. I managed to sneak an endotracheal tube through the open wound area, past the edge of the tightly pressed packing and directly into the open trachea. His airway was now open, but he was barely alive.

"I can't get a blood pressure reading at all," Ruth exclaimed. "I don't think he's going to make it." There was no argument from me. Still, you don't give up.

"Keep going!"

"Right!"

As we ran the gurney directly into the Operating Room, all three of us were so covered with splattered blood we looked like someone had thrown a kettle of ketchup over us. The OR team was ready, primed, and sprang into action.

Our responsibility was now back in the Emergency Room, so Ruth and I headed there, where a hasty shower and change of scrub suit, time permitting, would have us ready for the next catastrophe to present itself. Later that night the word came down from the OR. Incredibly, the man had survived. The LSU Surgery team had saved another one. There was little time to reflect upon this good news, however, for the ER "joint was jumping," as usual, with the ceaseless flow of people in critical situations of all kinds.

During one eight hour stretch in the ER, I recorded thirteen stab wounds with punctured lungs which required me to insert chest tubes, three gunshot wounds of the abdomen, three cardiac arrests, lacerations too numerous to count, one massive upper GI bleeder spewing out blood, one colon obstruction, one acute appendicitis, and more than two hundred acute asthmatics, (that is nearly one per minute, folks), various and sundry other things. As Ripley said, believe it or not.

Working in the Charity ER was akin to working in a circus, walking on an electrified high wire, the voltage always there; you never knew what the next moment would bring—an exhilarating, flaming emotional high with each success, or a crushing emotional descent with a defeat. It was high drama, and sometimes low comedy. Unlike the fisherman who can never be sure when or what the next catch might be, the Charity Hospital Emergency Room could be certain it would be in the next few moments, but *what* it would be was uncertain. Whether that next moment would be calamitous, comedic, heart-rending, joyful, sad, routine or unforgettable remained to be seen. You could be sure *something* was about to happen, though.

MEDICAL MIRACLE

Boudreaux

Early detection and intervention in cancer is critical to the likelihood of totally eradicating the malignancy. In other words, as Yogi Berra might expound, "If you don't show up until it's too late, it's too late to show up."

"Boudreaux" was trying not to be too late. Boudreaux was a twenty-two year old Louisiana Cajun, young and poor, a small but solid body with dark brown eyes and black hair. He was from deep in the bayou country, remote from busy urban civilization. When I walked into the examining room, he was bent over double by severe abdominal pain.

"When did your pains start? I asked. No answer. "How long have you been sick?" He glanced at me with a grimace, but continued his writhing posture, and did not reply.

"Look," I requested again, understanding his silence to be due to his all-consuming discomfort, "I know you are in severe pain, but I must find out what is going on. How did this start?"

With an straining effort he eked out, haltingly, the words, *"Parlez vous en Francais?"* The revelation came to me like the dawning of an awakening day's sunrise—*He speaks no English.*

"Mais oui," I replied. *"Je parle la Francais, mais certainement, petite. Quelle domage,"* a form of apology for my scarce knowledge of the French language.

By my few French phrases, our combined gestures and the able assistance of a French speaking Sister of Charity nun, we gathered essential information. Friends had driven him from his home in the bayou country near Lafayette. He had been hurting about twenty hours, with nausea and vomiting but no diarrhea. His pain had localized into his right lower abdomen over McBurney's point. Acute appendicitis was indicated by the physical findings and a substantiating white blood cell count of 21,000.

A copy of Boudreaux's old hospital records was requested, if there were any. Josh, my senior resident, came to check and approve my intended surgical intervention

On seeing who the patient was, Josh took me aside and said, "I know this patient, Ernie. I was involved in his case last year. It was weird. We opened this young guy and found out he had inoperable cancer all through his belly. He had hundreds of implants in his abdominal cavity. We took a lot of biopsies and Pathology reported it as widespread undifferentiated adenocarcinoma. Really rare in such a young guy, eh? Hard to believe. It was inoperable cancer, all we could do was close him. We were never sure where the cancer had started. It was a moot point anyway, because he was hopelessly terminal. It's a miracle he's lived this long."

A miracle, Josh said. A word that was about to prove prophetic to the extreme.

"Wow, that history surprises me, Josh. I thought he had all the signs of acute appendicitis. "

"Yeah, nothing you can do, though. I suppose it's possible, but highly unlikely, that a metastatic spreading cancer might obstruct the appendix lumen; that way it could possibly imitate or actually provoke an acute appendicitis, but that 's really stretching it. Cancer was found all over the place and he should have already been dead long ago. It's hard to believe he's made it this long. Boudreaux may finally be nearing a terminal state."

"But, Josh, don't you think it might be acute appendicitis in a patient who happens to also have cancer. Every sign of appendicitis is there. We can't ignore that. Boudreaux sure looks mighty healthy to be more than a year since inoperable abdominal cancer was found. Are you sure he's the same patient?"

"Oh, I remember him, Ernie, and it's right there in the chart. It was so unusual. He had a belly full of cancer implants. We presented the case at the Saturday conference because he was so young to have CA, using sigmoid colon as the probable diagnosis. Unusual to have it so advanced, too, at his age."

In Louisiana bayou country live many people descended from other people who migrated from the French-speaking area of eastern Canada in the early days of this country. They were called Arcadians, pronounced as *Ar-cad'-i-yonzes'* by the French. Over a period of time the word Arcadians was transformed, or Americanized by their new Louisiana neighbors into "Arcajuns," and thence into "Cajuns."

The Cajuns that appeared for care at Charity Hospital in New Orleans usually came for serious problems, referred by outlying smaller Charity Hospitals. They also came of their own accord. Many of the Cajun patients spoke only Cajun French and lived their entire life in the bayou country, never coming into English-speaking areas like New Orleans. The remoteness of their existence breeds inherent problems in their schooling and in health care, especially the delay in detecting cancer or seeking proper treatment for tetanus. Tetanus ("lockjaw") is a frequent cause of admission to Charity Hospital. Most tetanus cases come from the Cajun bayou areas because they do not get their protective immunization injections, despite being required by state law. During the years I was at Charity there was seldom a day that we did not have a "lockjaw" tetanus case in the intensive care unit. According to one report, fifty-five per cent of the "lockjaw" in the entire United States occurs in Louisiana. Curiously, the approximate same percentage was the cure rate in Louisiana. The relative high rate of cure in Louisiana, when compared to the near 100% fatalities in other states, is likely a function of Louisiana's greater experience in treating tetanus, and doing that treatment in one central collecting center.

"There was nothing we could do," Josh repeated. "Boudreaux simply had no chance."

"He sure has all the signs of acute appendicitis. "

As we talked, the records arrived. Sure enough, they confirmed his past cancer surgery just as Josh remembered. "Well," he said, "it may be an exercise in futility because of the innumerable cancer implants last year, but you might be right. Take him to surgery when he is prepped and ready. I'll come and take a look when you get inside."

"Okay.

At surgery, acute appendicitis was found and the appendix removed. Incredibly, and to the complete astonishment of both of us, there was absolutely no evidence of cancer or metastatic implants anywhere to be found in the entire abdomen cavity of organs. Josh had come up to see for himself this unbelievable development. The disappearance of the entire cancerous tissue could not be explained scientifically. And it never was.

In the ensuing research into the life of Boudreaux since his "inoperable" cancer a year earlier, nothing was ever determined that could account for the miraculous disappearance of the cancerous destruction within him. Boudreaux always claimed everyone praying for him, and

God's help, had caused the miracle. That was good enough for him, and good enough for me.

My decades of practicing medicine proved to me beyond any doubt that prayer does help, in many ways. In recent years Duke University and Stanford University have been reported as doing early research into prayers and their helpful place in selected medical cases.

THE LEGEND KNOWN AS TEX

An Unforgettable Character

Tex was a 6 foot 6 inch senior surgery resident with red hair, resplendent in his ever-present cowboy boots and surgical scrub suit. His huge fists required size nine and one-half surgical gloves, as opposed to the average size seven and one-half. Tex was usually quiet and reserved. When he did speak, it was a good idea to pay attention. He had a short-fuse temper.

This would get him in trouble with Charity Hospital of New Orleans administrators occasionally, each incident resulting in Tex being disciplined by a suspension from his residency for days or weeks, to be made up later at the end of his residency.

I suspected we might be about to have one of his famous incidents. Tex was beginning to boil about something. I could tell. His lips were pinched together, his face getting redder by the minute. It seemed certain Mount Vesuvius was building to another famous eruption.

"What's wrong, Tex?" He glanced my way, with a quizzical look, but said nothing, and returned to stare fixedly at his lunch of the hated red beans and rice, the repetitive diet every Wednesday—and it was Wednesday once again. Maybe I was wrong in my suspicions. Time would tell.

Red beans and rice. A Louisiana diet staple. Every Wednesday at Charity Hospital in New Orleans red beans and rice are offered as a meal to four hundred interns and residents, in one large room capable of handling, at best, two hundred persons at any given moment. These meals are to be gulped down amid noise that would drive a Baptist preacher to booze. The noise level would compare favorably to a chorus of perhaps fifty to a hundred discordant jackhammers blasting away in the room.

At the head of the room at a long table sit the VIP's—the administrators, trustees and chiefs of various departments such as anesthesiology, along with the occasional visiting dignitary. As these regal occupants faced the dilemma of their own red beans and rice, they were probably confident in their own minds, however, that the noise level was perhaps the result of two hundred jackasses, or certainly some even lower form of life.

Somewhere in this vast universe, I am certain, can be found many who have been groomed from childhood to accept as a steady diet red beans and rice as a tasty replacement, or substitute, for an entire meal. Not every palate is that strongly attuned. Some people may become *blasé* and settle for red beans and rice, rationalizing that nutrition of any kind is preferred to starvation. For all I know, some may choose to be buried in red beans and rice. Feel free, I say.

Others may quietly resign themselves to eat the repetitive dish over and over and accept their fate, not unlike the resignation of a condemned man, with no appeals left, walking to meet his doom. The strength of that resignation, however, can be expected to ebb away during the four or five years of one's training at the same institution, until a point of revulsion is eventually reached.

In my case, personally, I had reached that end point. To paraphrase Patrick Henry, "Give me the liberty of no red beans and rice or give me death." I just refused to eat any more red beans and rice, and usually skipped lunch on Wednesdays, but not today. I observed Tex mouthing unspoken words.

The interns and residents grumbled about red beans and rice, but there was nothing we could do to rectify it, doomed to Wednesday red beans and rice. We were licensed graduate doctors, but we were only lowly interns and residents, earning only twenty-five dollars a month, which confirmed in the minds of the administrators the legitimacy of our lowly station.

This particular Wednesday I sat at the lunch table, fasting, in order to avoid the red bean delicacy, and was just visiting with friends. The usual griping about the red beans and rice was traveling around the tables, however, not from the native Louisianans. Of course not, no self-respecting Louisianan would disparage their own lifestyle.

There were new arrivals coming to eat, and there were those departing. In the confusion of the massive exodus and arrivals, little attention was paid when Tex, whom I would come to call the "Legend," because of his many noteworthy incidents at Charity Hospital, arose with his newly filled plate of red beans and rice piled in a high, exaggerated mound, and casually ambled down the aisle. His direction took him past a number of other tables, as though he might be going to talk or visit with other residents at the tables toward the front of the room.

Tex did not stop to talk, or to sit at one of the other tables to visit. He continued past in a steady, purposeful and controlled pace, like a man on a mission. I watched with increasing fascination, as he came near the long table of the VIP administrators and the department chairmen. He came to a stop and paused in front of their table, looking directly at them until he had their full attention.

Calmly, as cool as an Eskimo in an igloo, Tex turned to a pedestal table upon which rested a wooden box. He lifted the lid of the box, which bore a label, "SUGGESTIONS", and dumped the entire contents of his plate piled high with the red beans and rice directly into the box. He proceeded to depart the room in the same calm manner, like any other executioner after the deed is done.

There was a moment of complete silence, then an instant cheering and chattering burst out, accompanied by applause, followed by a tidal wave of laugher rippling around the room, as the news spread like a fire in a dry forest about what Tex had just done.

The red beans and rice continued, however a few alternative side choices appeared from time to time. I am not certain if Tex received any days of suspension, but by his action he made many new fans of those who approved his action—predominantly among the anti-red bean and rice crowd, obviously.

The administrators finally decided to take no more chances. They removed the Suggestion Box.

✽ ✽ ✽

The blaring loudspeaker just above our heads was barking out a continuous stream of names, interns and residents being paged. In the echoing confines of the hospital lunchroom, the loud paging continued nonstop, name after name. Combined with the clatter of dishes and the loud talking, it sounded like a hundred discordant automatic rifles or air-operated hammers going full blast. You could hardly hear yourself speak. In addition there were lighted panels flashing the paging numbers of doctors unceasingly, each of the four hundred doctors being sought having a different number. Seemingly, this should have been enough in itself, without the additional continuous squawking of the loudspeaker box.

The 3000 bed hospital was approved for 450 residents and interns As a result, the lunchroom was usually packed, even if only half of the staff were there at any one time. with the combination of conversation, clatter of dishes, and scraping of benches, creating a loud echoing, buzzing sound, adding to the fierce, piercing sounds of the continuous loudspeaker, the room could have easily passed for an auditory torture chamber for interrogation purposes.

Tex fidgeted next to me, picking at his dinner plate, red beans and rice again, his face clouding up more by the minute. Tension was building, mine from watching Tex in the throes of his accelerating discontent and anger, from causes unknown to me. I knew something was cooking in Vesuvious, but had no idea what.

At the front of the huge lunchroom, at the special table reserved for them, sat the same VIP's—the administrator, the hospital's section chiefs and the occasional trustee board members, and a couple of visiting politicians.

Without a word of explanation to me or anyone, Tex arose. He walked calmly over and ripped the bolted loudspeaker from the walls, sauntered to the front of the now silent room under the gaze of all eyes, deposited the quieted speaker atop the pedestal table which formerly held the Suggestion Box, under the gaped countenance of all the VIP's at their table only ten feet away. Tex proceeded back to his lunch table amid the quiet, which erupted into applause, laughter and cheers. Joy reigned. The loudspeaker was never replaced.

❈ ❈ ❈

Although Tex may not have been required to make up any time for his "red beans and rice" or "loudspeaker" incidents, he certainly was for the big incident which occurred about a month later.

The big suspension came from an unlikely event. Tex was asked by the OB-Gyn department to hurriedly see, as a surgery emergency, a female patient of the gynecology service, as time was of the essence in her case. Tex hastened to the ward of the patient, only to find she was on a bedpan, in the process of emptying her intestinal tract preparatory to immediate surgery. Tex assisted the patient in the removal of the filled bedpan.

Tex looked around. There was no immediate place to deposit the bedpan, but Tex spotted an employee of the hospital nearby, lazily mopping the floor.

"Could you help me with this, please?" He extended the bedpan. "This lady has to go to emergency surgery right away, and I have to examine her in a hurry."

The employee stopped mopping, leaned upon his mop handle, tilted his head toward Tex, and replied defiantly, "I just mops." At last, the chance had come to express his own individuality, like the low man on any totem-pole syndrome, or pecking order, who finally gets the opportunity to exert his influence. The mopper was enjoying himself at the doctor's expense, not realizing he was delaying the urgent care of the patient.

Taking time to kindly explain, Tex asked again, "This nice black lady is desperately sick and needs surgery quickly. There is no place for me to put this bedpan, and no time to spare. How about helping out and taking care of it, to save time and help this lady?" This was probably more words than he had said at any one time in the last week.

"Nope, my job is to mop. I done told you, I just mops." He continued to lean on his mop, disinterested, but smug and pleased with his control of the situation.

"What!" Tex fired back, "You won't help this lady of your own race?"

Shaking his head from side to side, holding his unchanged posture, the man replied indignantly, "I'm telling you, I just mops." He continued to lean his chin upon his folded hands atop the mop handle.

With that, Tex had enough and shouted, "Well, dammit, go ahead and *mop*!" He lifted the bedpan and tossed it into the air. Torrents of the contents gushed out, splattering upon the floor, followed shortly by the bed pan hitting the floor. A cascading shower of odorous liquid and solid material flew in every direction. Tex returned to helping his critically ill patient.

The outcome? The patient was taken to surgery immediately. Her life was saved, but Tex got a big suspension, was forced to apologize to the employee, a task that set him fuming once again. He swallowed his anger enough to get through it, but, knowing Tex as I did, it had to be a close call for the employee not to experience another "incident." Perhaps, the employee also learned something of value from his experience: "an ounce of prevention can prevent *more* than a pound of trouble." It can certainly prevent a bedpan full of trouble.

I have often wondered how long Tex had to hang around at the end of his residency, making up time for his suspensions. I am aware, however, that Tex went on to become a distinguished surgeon and taught surgery to many others. His skill with his hands in the operating room places him as one of the two or three best I ever encountered,—and as a surgeon myself, I observed many. I wonder if he still wears his cowboy boots. Yep!

TEN YEARS OF RAPE

―•―

Case Of The Egg Girl

In this particular case, a 19 year-old girl with dyed blonde hair, blue eyes and a slow intellect, reported to the police about ten to fourteen days after participating in what she had later decided was rape. When brought to me for evaluation, she began her incredible story.

"I was just out walking 'bout midnight a week or two ago, you know, across that bridge over I-75 up by the Farmer's Market. You know the one I mean?" To encourage her to continue, I nodded affirmatively.

"Well," she continued, "this boy I know came by in his car and asked where I was going. I said to the farmer's market. He said he was too, and said hop in, so I did. You know that building where they check eggs to see if they is alright?"

"Yes, I do." It was adjacent to a popular restaurant at the Farmer's Market.

"Well, we went in there and was hanging out in that building for a while, you know, talking with a bunch of his friends. Then he said let's go upstairs, and we did. It was real dark up there and we started fooling around, you know, and after a while we got real hot, so we laid down on this cot and had sex. Then, he went down stairs." At that point it sounded like a spontaneous tryst and nothing to suggest rape. I remained silent, to see if she had more to say. She was on a roll and the information was flowing. Any questions could come later.

"A few minutes later, he come back, and we had sex again in the dark, then he left me again and went back down stairs. At this point, I interrupted. "It sounds to me like you were agreeing to have sex, instead of rape. Is that right?"

"Wait a minute, you ain't heard it all yet." She stirred in her seat, obviously vexed with my attempt at a hasty conclusion.

"I'm sorry, continue."

"Well, a few minutes later, you know, he comes back in that dark room again and we have sex and he goes back down stairs again, see. Ever little while, he'd come back and have sex again, until we done had sex ten or twelve times."

This staggered my imagination. If true, I thought, perhaps a Guinness record. Such prodigious endurance would be incredible. The average male would be left in a near-moribund state of exhausted frustration attempting to match the virile young man's endurance, also decidedly envious of such prowess. A deep suspicion began; another more logical explanation seemed likely.

"That was more than a week or so ago, why is it that you have waited until now to decide that you were raped?" Was she that slow mentally, or was there some other underlying process at work of which I was yet to be informed?

"Cause he don't like me no more, and I just found out he wern't the only one having sex with me; not ever single time I had sex, anyway. It was all them others taking turns, too." Suspicion confirmed. Poor girl, not excessively bright, had been sharing a series of sexual encounters, as if a revolving door was spitting out partners in a regular rotation.

"Are you telling me that you could not tell the difference, in any kind of way, between the all the different young men?" That would be difficult to believe, a hard pill to swallow.

"Nah, I couldn't tell no diff"rence. That's why I decided it's rape. It is, ain't it?"

I left that question unanswered. It was difficult enough just controlling an urge to laugh out loud at the absurdity of her statement. I examined her in the usual prescribed manner, and informed her that the District Attorney, with the help of the police, would sort this situation out and give her answers to her questions. Unlike the myriad of other cases, I was never called to testify in this case, as it never came to court.

Her case is only one of several to be discussed, as examples of the broad variety of rape cases that came my way. The gamut ran from brutal tragedy to high comedy, from criminal to revengeful recriminations, from hysteria to fantasy.

My ten years experience examining 100% of all alleged rape and real rape cases in the Clayton County area of Metropolitan Atlanta, as well as some of the cases from adjoining counties, came about in a peculiar, roundabout way.

A prisoner died of a heart attack in the Clayton County jail. The Atlanta Journal and Constitution newspaper crackled with rebuke and scorn on page one, with justifiable fiery criticism of the county administration for having no program of medical attention in the jail, nor for any other matters of official county government concerns as well. This escalating bonfire of flaming media criticism lit a fire under the commissioner's coattails.

The commissioners of Clayton County, one of the five counties making up Greater Atlanta, appointed me to represent the county on official medical matters and gave me the grand official title of Clayton County Physician. This was in addition to my private practice, of course. About the same time I was also serving as the physician member of the Hospital Authority to build the new, modern Clayton General Hospital, (later to be renamed the Southern Regional Medical Center of Atlanta). The possibility of my examining and evaluating rape cases had never entered my mind, but the acceptance of one responsibility often leads to another.

At first, in my new capacity, I examined all new prisoners, made regular rounds upon the inmates, and attended to their regular medical needs as well as any emergency needs that might arise at the jail. Some emergencies, if deemed appropriate, could be brought to my office one block away.

The first call to me, regarding a *rape* case, came one night about 1:00 A.M. The detectives were at the Emergency Clinic of our new hospital with a lady rape victim. Previously, this case would have been taken to Grady Memorial Hospital in downtown Atlanta, who then would bill Clayton County for the medical expenses, but Grady now refused because Clayton had it's own new facility.

The detective informed me the lady had her own personal gynecologist doctor (an M.D. specialist who treats only the female reproductive system). The detective had telephoned, but the doctor had refused to come see his patient, for fear of having to come to court and be legally involved. "Doc, since Clayton General Hospital policy won't let the ER doctors get involved, we called you because you are now the Official Clayton County Physician. What do we do?"

Somebody, I thought, has to step up there and be counted for that unfortunate lady;—for the sake of the medical profession, too. No further consideration was necessary. "I guess it'll have to be me. I'll be there in about twenty minutes." Unknowingly, those words would lead to ten years of examining every possible alleged rape case in our county's portion of Metropolitan Atlanta, as well as some cases from adjoining Henry County and Fayette County.

It was difficult for me to understand how a woman's personal physician, particularly a gynecologist, could so casually abandon his patient in such a dire time of her need. That attitude was new to me at the time. This kind of selfish thinking and total disregard for the revered Oath of Hippocrates was to spread among the new breed of doctors and would explain much of the erosion of respect for the medical profession that has come to pass in the ensuing years.

Every imaginable type of situation involving rape or alleged rape came my way, along with various emotional and psychological consequences. How can I possibly convey the misery and pathos, the destructive psychological effects, and some times the brutality many these poor innocent ladies underwent? How can I explain adequately ten years of an emotional roller-coaster ride of emotions I underwent with each of these unfortunate people? In my role as examiner, I became as well counselor, psychologist, minister, psychotherapist, and supportive friend. I ran the gamut of emotions from sadness, grief, horror, incredulity, rejection, derision, depression, and yes, sometimes even laughter. I have been threatened, spit upon, attacked, cursed and ignored, but rarely thanked or praised for my assistance.

The Egg Girl, as well as the following few, varied representative cases may be the best means available for the reader to gain a semblance of understanding. Unless the reader has been preyed upon forcibly and personally experienced the horror of brutal rape, no written words of which I am aware can truly give the reader a full depth of understanding, not only of the physical damage, but also of the crushing, debilitating damage to the mental makeup and psyche.

CASE OF THE MALL SHOPPER

The young lady was in her mid-to late twenties. She had been shopping at the SouthLake Mall. She completed her shopping and departed the stores just prior to the closing time of the major stores. She walked towards her car in a less than well-lighted area. She thought nothing of a van approaching along the same lane until it suddenly stopped beside her and two men jumped out from the opened side door and grabbed her, pulling her into the van immediately, her packages scattering upon the ground. She had time only to scream briefly. No help came.

The two men held her in the back of the van, while a third man was driving. She said she kept screaming and that is when the men began to beat her in the face, cursing her and yelling her to shut up, as they ripped at her clothing. She tried kicking at them, and only received more beating as a result. They taped her mouth and wrists with gray duct tape. She said the van stopped somewhere in a dark area, probably wooded, she could not see outside. Two of them held her legs while the third held her arms down and forcibly raped her, then each took his turn similarly. As the third arose from her supine position, the first man who had beaten her face so brutally stepped above her and urinated, spraying all over her, the final crushing demeaning act. They drove the van to another area and pushed her out along a roadside where she had been rescued by a motorist and the police called.

This was the story as she related it to me while sobbing in the examination room. She had a blanket covering her torn clothing fragments and battered body. Physical examination revealed scattered, multiple scratches and severe bruises of her face and extremities, chest and abdomen. Despite my usual professional front, I always cried inside for these poor victimized women, and seethed in anger at their assailants, who disgrace the human race. The gynecological evaluation confirmed that forcible entry had occurred, supported also by internal and external evidence as well as lab studies. The history and the examination were compatible with rape, now it was up to the detective and the courts to prove it was rape, and by whom. My testimony as to the positive and corroborating evidence would be required in court.

COMMENT: If possible, ladies need to shop in the daytime, preferably with a friend. Park in areas where many cars are parked, where many people are walking to and fro. Be alert at all times to your immediate environment, as to what may be a threat to your safety possibly developing anywhere in your vicinity. Your best chance for escape is in the first few seconds or minutes. Otherwise, in most cases, once you are "captured" physically, I would advise not fighting, some rapists anticipate it and are stimulated by attempts at resistance as an excuse to be brutal. Sometimes, this can result in a death. If you are able, keep your wits about you, expend energy observing and collecting every bit of evidence you can in order for the police to apprehend and imprison the rapist forever.

Case Of The Barbcue Fork And The Narc Agent

The detectives brought a hysterical, sobbing and screaming young lady into my office. Mascara was smeared all about her eyes like the mask of a second-story burglar, or a raccoon. Her shrieking voice was shouting confused, rambling accusations as two detectives and a police officer tried to restrain her. Patients in the reception area were upset and frightened by the noisy disruption. Her arms flailed this way and that in agitated movements, her words incoherently mixed with babblings about rape, barbecue forks, "them," and other unintelligible words, including some man's unintelligible name. Trying to get her under control was proving a formidable task. To take a statement or do a physical exam was appearing nigh impossible. I was relieved when the officers finally maneuvered her into a private examining room, where the ranting and raving continued.

The officers and I were deciding what to do next when suddenly the door to the room burst open, slamming against the wall with a crash. A long-haired, scruffy-looking man with a golden earring was the culprit. He appeared to be in his late twenties, unshaven, with wild eyes and a long pony-tail streaming down his back. He was dressed in jeans and flowered shirt. He pushed the door against the wall again with another loud bang. Shoving me aside physically, he pointed at me and yelled at the detectives, "Get this clown out of here !"

I was startled, to say the least. It was *my* office. As a young lad I had worked as a laborer for Ringling Brothers, Barnum and Bailey, and several other circuses, but never as a clown, and I resented his inference. The detectives were embarrassed. They grabbed at the young man to restrain him, talking to him, trying to calm him down. Their hands were full, trying to handle him and the woman at the same time.

"Barry," they shouted, as he fought their grasps, "this is Doctor Abernathy, the Official Clayton County Physician and the police surgeon, he's got to examine her."

"I don't give a damn who he is, get him the hell out of here."

The detective looked apologetically at me, hunched his shoulders up, spread his arms with his palms up in a gesture of indecisive surrender, asking forgiveness. He stepped close to me and said softly, "Doc, I'm sorry about this guy's behavior. He's an undercover Narc, and that is his girlfriend, and he's just real upset."

"That's no excuse for busting into my office like some wild braying jackass, slamming doors and scaring everybody in the building."

"I'm really sorry, doc. I hate to ask you this, but if you don't mind, will you step outside the room so we can get him calmed down and then maybe we can get things done. Okay?"

I did not like being shoved. I did not like being called a clown, nor did I relish yielding to the Narc's order to leave my own examining room, but I understood the detective's predicament, so I relented and said, reluctantly, "Okay."

After a semblance of calm was restored, the story unfolded. The woman claimed that certain of the Narc's "associates" (addicts? dealers?) had broken into the apartment, beaten and raped her physically and then repeated the act with a huge wooden handled barbecue fork, leaving it in her vagina when they departed. A bizarre story, but not yet the most bizarre I would encounter. The routine examination was finally completed and uneventful, no physical findings of special note. Lab data would become available later. The police department helped the young Narc and his hysterical girlfriend to find a new secret "safe house" apartment, unknown to anyone, and life went on.

About two weeks later, guess who was brought in, hysterical, to repeat the exact same story, supposedly raped while living in the absolutely new, perfectly-hidden "safe house" apartment; raped physically by the same men as before, and then raped again with a huge barbecue fork, again, which was again left in place in her vagina when the men left. No physical evidence was ever ascertained to corroborate the stories. I was never called to testify, which speaks volumes, as *unspoken* words, I suppose.

Case Of The Police Station Rape

I came to dread the televised talk shows about rape, with the panel of ladies sitting prim and proper, as they preened before the camera discoursing on the subject of rape. Undoubtedly, they were well-meaning in their endeavors, but unaware they often were informing potential rapists of new ways to inflict their desires on unsuspecting innocent victims, as well as ways to safeguard their crimes.

For instance, I witnessed one particular televised show where the panel described in detail a technique whereby a woman driving alone could have her car bumped from behind intentionally. Getting out of the car to check possible damage, the woman has now taken the first desired step and is now vulnerable. The talk show ladies continued to give more specific instruction. If the woman is not taken at that moment of encounter, the would-be rapist is sizing her up for consideration. He then follows the woman's car to some place he deems more appropriate and safer in which to corner her, such as a lonely road or street, sometimes even her own driveway, and forces his sexual attentions upon her. Almost immediately, I had the first of several rape cases involving the rear bumper technique, the most revolting I call the "police station/city hall rape."

The blonde lady, about middle thirties, had stopped about 1:00 A.M. in the morning at a major traffic light intersection in the village of Jonesboro, the county seat of Clayton County. The traffic light was on North Main Street at the junction of Georgia highway 3 and Highway 54, and well lighted. Her car was struck lightly from behind. She got out to inspect for damage. Two black men also emerged from the car behind her. To everyone's apparent relief, no significant damage was found. After a few words of conversation, the lady became troubled by the coarseness of the men's suggestive language. She resumed her drive, but noticed the car stayed close behind her, following her each turn she took. In her panic, she drove to the nearest police station location which she could recall, only three blocks away down the same street as she was driving.

She pulled her car in front of the building shared by Jonesboro City Hall and the Jonesboro Police Station and parked, thinking she would be safe, unaware they were closed at night. Only one patrolman in a roving car was on duty at night in Jonesboro in those days. The building was a small one-story building located on the *north* side of a narrow, dark side street which separated it from the huge Clayton County Courthouse. The large and efficient Clayton County Police Force, however, is the powerful police force for the entire county and has its major facility, as well as the county jail, brightly lighted on the *south* side of the courthouse, only one hundred yards away, with scores of police cars and officers busily working.

The two men following her car pulled directly behind her automobile effectively blocking it from being able to back out or move. Sadly, they both subsequently raped her right at that location, in front of the Jonesboro Police station and City Hall building, less than one hundred yards from safety. Jonesboro now has a new, large modern police station manned by more officers and efficient personnel in an improved location.

Be certain, I am not faulting efforts by the televised panels of concerned ladies, trying to inform other women about the dangers of rape and how to protect yourself against rape. I approve of it heartily, but the rash of rear bumper cases of rape I examined immediately after their graphic description points out the need to be careful about outlining possible techniques for "wannabe" rapists.

Among my ten years of experience in rape and alleged rape there were husbands or boyfriends accused by married or single ladies who were mad and fabricated the whole event for revenge, divorcing wives who just made it up for punishment, young girls from age eight years old and up, one child only 6 years old, one case who came back with friends and robbed my office, one with gonorrhea who falsely accused me in order to try to avoid paying for a bill, one suspected rape-murder case found dead in a river, hands tied behind her back and drowned.

Case Of A Man Raped

A young man named Lance, 27 years of age, with exaggerated mannerisms and readily-apparent "tanned" facial makeup presented with complaints of rectal bleeding, which he said occurred after a constipated bowel movement. Examination revealed suspicious lacerated tears, and severely swollen hemorrhoids. His demeanor was quite effeminate. When confronted with my suspicions, he changed his story.

"Well, alright. It happened while I was in New York City a few days ago. Actually, I was gang raped." He waved his hands about with a flourish, brushed his dyed blonde hair back as he made a tossing motion with his head. He then struck a stance of unconcern, staring steadily at me.

"Did you report it to the New York Police?"

"No, it wouldn't have done any good. The men were strangers to me, I only knew their first names. Anyway, I had a plane to catch early the next morning, and had no time for all that jazz."

"Besides my private practice," I told him, "I am the official County Physician. In that capacity, I am responsible for all possible rape cases," He became alert at that news. "I may have to report this, although I doubt it, because of the New York jurisdiction. Better tell me the details, in case I need them later."

He deliberated a moment, thought it over, and said, "Why not? What do I care? I decided to visit this gay bar in lower Manhattan bar that my friends had raved about. They said it was terrible notorious and exciting, and I should visit it while in New York, so I did. When I entered the front door, the décor was just fabulous. It was very crowded. Everything you could imagine was happening there, I mean, *really*." Looking me up and down, he added, "Some things hard for *you* to believe, I mean right in front of everybody, there was sexy things happening." He tilted his head at me for emphasis, raising his eyebrows and said, "For goodness sakes, just use your imagination, silly. This was a gay bar." As he spoke, he pursed his lips is a suggestive pose. I already had used my imagination, and now it appeared I was undoubtedly correct in my earlier assumption.

"Then what happened?"

"My new friends that I met at the bar were very pleasant, and we had several drinks together. It didn't take long for sexual topics to enter the conversation. I mean, with all the open sexual activities going on all around me, what would you expect? Lots of suggestive talk and touching, you know, as one drink followed another." He stopped, fixed his gaze upon me, probing, asking, "Are you married, Doctor? I don't see a ring."

"Yes, I am. Never mind. Continue." My interview searching for facts was beginning to be joined by an ounce of vicarious curiosity.

He looked directly at me again, made a slight tug at his pants, as men will have to do from time to time, as if to straighten them when they become bunched uncomfortably at the crotch. A signal I ignored. He looked a little longer, then shrugged, and continued, "Well, the night went into the wee hours. My newfound drinking friends were becoming very aggressive in their touching and their talk." He paused, took a long breath slowly, looked into my eyes suggestively, questioning. His message was clear enough, but I was not of his persuasion, and ignored his implied inquiry.

Realizing his story was not precipitating or provoking in my face any show of shock or stimulated interest, he decided to draw his tale to a precipitant close. "Almost before I knew what was happening, they had me bent me over a barroom table. Many of the men in the rest of the room stopped what they were doing and watched. They cheered and some laughed as I was raped anally and brutally by both of them taking turns." He looked deep into my eyes to gauge the effect of his dramatic finish. "End of story. Would you mind terribly if I had a cigarette?" His attempt to provoke me had failed.

Did I believe his story as told? Did it matter whether he was truly forcibly raped, or a voluntary participant subjected to a more forceful and hurtful situation than he had anticipated, a dangerous mistake? That was a moot question, in addition to the jurisdictional considerations. Did he claim it was rape in an attempt to spare his embarrassment with a physician unknown to him, or did he even care about embarrassment, or was he deliberately confronting me with his persuasion and trying to shock, embarrass or entice me? It mattered not. His medical care *was* of importance, and I proceeded.

"Medically, I shall care for your wounds and instruct you as to what you must do. Though I am certainly no lawyer, my experience suggests you have no practical legal course of action under the circumstances, however that is left up to legal authorities, not me."

When surgery for his prolapsed bleeding hemorrhoids was completed and he returned to the office for follow up, he had an unexpected surprise. "Lance," I said, "There is good news and bad news. First, the bad news. I am sorry to inform you that your friends did even more to you than you knew. Your pathology lab tests actually showed active spirochetes in your hemorrhoid tissue." I paused to observe his response.

"What does that mean?" He visibly was nervous now, not the same flippant persona he had flaunted earlier.

"You have syphilis, a serious venereal disease." He was shocked, arising from his chair, his mouth agape. "You are very lucky to find it out this early, because it is likely too early for blood tests to show if it was contracted in New York so recently."

"You call that lucky, are you crazy:" Lance was getting his bravado act together again.

"Despite what you may think, yes, your are lucky to find it out so early. More bad news, Georgia law requires the doctor to report it to the State. Now, the good news. Syphilis can be treated successfully. The earlier treatment starts, the better chances are for a good result."

"When can I start? Lance was anxious, his former cavalier attitude no longer existing, only a memory.

"We' will draw the blood sample and start treatment right now." And we did.

Case Of Court Testimony

Of all the court testimonies I recall, my favorite possibly, as a result of courtroom audience participation, is an alleged rape victim of questionable intellect who had revenge on her mind. Her findings had been negative, her story highly doubtful. It had already been established that she had voluntarily gone to the tryst and had removed her own clothes. The case should probably never have come to court in the first place. Nevertheless, the Assistant District Attorney, trying to make a name for himself, had pushed her on the witness stand to a climactic crisis, where he was trying to elicit from the witness precise words to describe exactly what the man had done after her clothes were removed. The DA had developed his interrogation to the point where things had proceeded pleasantly to the moment of her impending entry and conjugal consummation.

"Then, *exactly* what did he do?" the district attorney demanded in a loud voice, anxious to have the jury hear the dramatic and fateful words to assure a conviction.

"Why, he raped me." The courtroom echoed a few quiet snickers and muffled laughter.

"Strike that from the record, please," he directed the court reporter. Returning to the subject, he took a slow, deep breath. In a soft voice of encouragement, he pleaded, "No, no. You can't say that. You are drawing a conclusion. The court has to decide the question of rape. Just say in your own words exactly what he did physically. Would you do that now, please? Then, *what* did he do?"

She bit her lips, fluttered her eyelids a few times. She twisted in the chair nervously, unable to bring herself to say the common four-letter word familiar to her, her scant vocabulary limiting any word as a substitute. Not a word did she utter. The room was silent, everyone straining to hear the reply, on the edge of their seats in lascivious anticipation.

"Speak, answer me," he began to roar, losing his cool, "what did he do? Speak out! You didn't make the whole thing up, so tell the jury, right now. What did he then do? Speak," he exhorted. He than lost his patience completely, "Can you maybe just say *what* he put exactly *where* he put it?"

The giggling and scattered laughter became a chorus in the courtroom. The DA glanced behind him at the courtroom and back at the judge, realizing he might have just gone a bit too far. The judge was scowling at him. Quickly, he faced the court reporter and added, "Strike that last sentence from the record, please." The judge remained silent, for which the prosecutor was thankful.

No answer had yet come from the woman in the witness box. Trying to provoke an answer, the DA put his face within inches of her face and snarled, "WHAT DID HE THEN DO?" Calming down from his frustration, and realizing she need help, he leaned close to her and said softly, trying to give her a way to express herself, "Look, if you can't think of a word that won't embarrass you, just use tab "A" and slot "B" to describe what he put where. Okay?"

The courtroom exploded with laughter at his tab "A" and slot "B" useage. He looked up, startled, as the judge pounded his gavel and demanded quiet in the courtroom. He rebuked the DA for his rhetoric, and demanded there will be no more of that.

The judge turned to the young woman and said, kindly, "You will have to answer the question, as best you can, young lady."

She remained silent in the witness box, but not still. In a slow rhythm she leaned forwards and backwards, wringing her hands as though washing them. Her face shone with perspiration. It was obvious she was struggling to come up with an answer other than the familiar, vernacular four-letter word. As I watched, I saw her facial expression change from one of despair to an accelerating look of triumph, replacing the confused countenance.

Her face beamed as she lifted her head up, faced the DA, and proudly announced for the whole courtroom to clearly hear, "He intercoursed me." The entire courtroom burst into loud, long laughter at the continuing comedic saga.

The judge pounded his gavel again, demanding silence. The DA's already doubtful case surely was lost now. And it was, as events ultimately proved, her testimony a final nail driven in the coffin of her dubious accusation.

These cases are only a few representative "sexamples" of the many and varied cases of rape and alleged rape cases when came by way during the ten years. "A Different Kind Of Rape" is presented in this collection. It seemed to deserve a solitary presentation.

A Different Kind Of Rape

"Jeez, Doc, I need a tranquilizer or something, and I need it right now." His facial countenance agreed with his self-diagnosis.

He was a well-known, prominent lawyer, whom I shall call Charles, also well known for his penchant for the ladies. His face and rumpled shirt were sweaty, despite the autumn cool weather. He was pale and very distraught, as he paced the office floor, licking his lips and casting nervous, furtive glances at me.

"Charles," I asked, "what seems to be the trouble?" A brilliant, innovative beginning.

"Doc, you wouldn't believe it, if I told you." A feint toward safety and non-revealment?

"Well, you might try me. You would be surprised at what I have sometimes had to believe." He really wants to tell me, I presume, or he would not have come this far.

"Why do you think you have this sudden need for tranquilizers?"

"Doc, I don't just think, I *know*. I am lucky to be alive this morning."

"Enlighten me."

Charles rubbed his index finger alongside his nose, lowered the hand until it grasped his chin and then his neck in a soft squeeze, like the motion of using a wash cloth. Is he trying unconsciously to wash away some kind of guilt, I wondered.

"Okay, but this is the strangest thing that has ever happened to me, and the *scariest* by far." He sat down in a chair as he spoke, could not remain there, and stood up again as he began to pour out his tale.

"Don't worry, anything you tell me will be kept in complete confidence."

"I'm not worried about that, Doc. I may tell it myself, later, after I calm down."

"Well, lay it out for me if you wish, and we shall see about possible tranquilizers."

He began, "I was over in north Atlanta last night, at the Falcon-Brave lounge. You know, the one at Cheshire Bridge Road named after the Atlanta Falcons and The Atlanta Braves.

"I know where you mean."

"I was having a few drinks at the bar, and I met this gorgeous girl with long black hair and beautiful eyes. God, what a figure—great big bazooms up front. You know what I mean?" He looked at me for understanding, wiggling his eyebrows up and down for emphasis, while cupping his hands in front of his chest, as if holding imaginary grapefruits.

"I know exactly what you mean, Charles. She was a lovely creature."

"Exactly. We had several drinks and things were going real well. When it got later, she said she had to go, but I could come with her to her apartment. I was all steamed up by this time and thanking my lucky stars for the chance to go with her. You know, expecting big things to happen by being invited."

"Yes, that would be a most natural assumption."

"We got to her apartment, and she invited me inside. Things were really looking good for me, as we had a drink or two of vodka." His tongue protruded and wiped his lips as he recalled the event, almost as if he could taste the excitement of that moment again.

His story was beginning to sound like another trite male *bragadoccio* event, and I began to prepare myself to feign genuine surprise or envy, whichever I could deem he was seeking.

"To make a long story shorter, Doc, we ended up in her bed, both of us naked as a couple of horny Jaybirds."

"If that is the end of your story, I don't see why you need a tranquilizer. Did she have a disease, AIDS or something, and you are scared?"

"No, Doc, nothing like that. When I reached over to touch her, she put her hand under her pillow. I thought maybe she was gonna get a condom out, but she pulled out a .357 Magnum pistol, Doc, pointed it, up close, right at my genitals. It looked like a cannon, Doc. It scared the bejeezus out of me." He grimaced at the memory. If caught in a similar situation, I would have, too.

She said, "Now, you sunnofabitch, you 're going to lay right here beside me all night and if you touch me any time during this night, I am going to blow your balls and dick clean away. If you don't believe me, you just try it." She pointed the weapon at his genital area for emphasis, to show she meant every word.

"That had to be a terrible position in which to find yourself." It surely was, for Charles enjoyed the reputation of being what is locally called, to put it politely, a womanizer. This had to be a real shocker for him, held in that position by a demented female on some kind of a personal crusade.

"You said it, Doc. I was really scared—I might fall asleep and accidentally touch her, you know. As it was, I was so terrified I remained wide awake all night, laying naked beside this naked woman with a big pistol, afraid I might fall asleep and roll over and touch her, or the gun might go off by accident if *she* fell asleep."

"What happened?"

"Morning light came and there we were, just like we had been all night, laying in the bed totally naked. I asked if I could go to the bathroom, scared as I have ever been at what might happen next. She didn't say one word, just waved that big pistol back and forth. Finally, I had to go so bad, I began to ease out of the bed real slowly, expecting to be shot any second. Walking toward the bathroom, the hairs on the back of my neck stood out, as I broke out in a cold sweat, fearing the impact of a bullet in my back at any second. I could just feel that big pistol pointing at me."

"Obviously, you made it out of there safely, or you wouldn't be here, right?"

"Wait, a minute, Doc, you got to hear the rest."

"Okay, so ahead."

"She got out of bed and stood over me, swinging that big gun at my privates, as I dressed. She followed right behind me to the door, and she actually stuck the cold barrel tip of the pistol into my back just as I got near the door. Doc, I thought I was going to meet my maker right then. My knees crumbled. I nearly fell flat down on the floor. She never said a word. I managed to finally reach the door, slowly opened it and gratefully eased through, still scared, not sure I was safe from being shot, even then, by this crazy woman. I closed the door slowly, as we stared each other in the face. She never said a word as the door closed. Doc, I ran. I mean, I ran as fast as I was able in my nervous condition, stumbling down that balcony and stairway, got in my car and drove straight here. I am still shaking inside and lucky to be alive. Now, you know why I need a tranquilizer."

"I believe I would too, Charles, if I had lived through something like that."

"Doc, I need a note for the court, too. I am in no shape to appear in court today, and try a case." It was going to take quite some time for Charles to recover from the rape of his self-esteem, I thought. You could call it a case of soul rape or spirit rape, I suppose.

Charles got the needed tranquilizer, and the note. He also got a valuable lesson.

SNAKEHANDLERS

―•―

SNAKES   CASE #1: RATTLESNAKES AND RELIGION

The lights flickering through the dining room window of my home indicated a car was coming down the driveway. It was about eleven o'clock at night, a little late for friends to come calling, but just right for another unusual case to present itself, maybe another rape case to handle. The alternating blue lights had informed me it was the police.

The knock on the door was not necessary, my hand was already on the handle to open it and greet my callers.

"Doc," Detective Brown said, "we got a kid in the other car, bit by a snake. He looks like he's about to die."

"Let's take a look at him." I walked out to a second automobile, a weathered and worn older van. A peek inside revealed a lad about ten or twelve years old, drawn up in a fetal position, unresponsive to my spoken inquiries, pale as a ghost except in an area where his face and neck were already blackened by the death of tissue. A similar area was present on his arm. The child appeared moribund, in the waning moments of life.

Turning to the detective and the three adults who arrived in the van, I asked, "Does anybody know what kind of snake it was, and when did it happen?"

The three adults remained silent. This unusual response raised my suspicions. I turned to Detective Brown, with a questioning look, my eyebrows arched.

"Doc," he said, "they said it was a rattlesnake, and it bit him on the neck, and face, but he was holding several other snakes at the same time, including a copperhead, and they ain't really too sure which snake, or how many, bit him.

That explained the blackened tissue. The venom of rattlesnakes is histiolytic,—(hist refers to cells, lytic refers to lysis or bursting)—meaning it bursts blood cells and arteries, depriving tissues of oxygen as the venom spreads. Tissues of muscles and tendons may die directly from contact with the venom, but mainly the loss is the result of losing a blood supply and oxygen. Extensive swelling and discoloration from cell death results, demanding immediate treatment and usually surgical fasciotomy. (opening the entire regional area with long incisions). The myth that rattlesnakes will make a "buzz" with their rattle before striking is not true. Rattlesnakes do not always rattle before they strike. Rattlesnakes come in many varieties, and exist throughout the Americas, from Canada to Argentina. They live about ten to twelve years, except for a few in captivity that have lived twenty or more years.

"You said several snakes at the same time? Why would anybody be doing a crazy thing as stupid as that?"

I looked at the three men for an answer, but received no comment. The tall man with a mustache, wearing a plaid shirt, shifted his feet nervously and looked uncomfortable. There was a very worried look of anxious concern on the face of a middle-aged man in overalls. I wondered if he was the father of the child. An especially stern countenance of the third man in a dark coat and wearing glasses was a striking exception. His face was set in rigid lines of defiance, his mouth a thin compressed horizontal line.

Turning to Brown, I asked, "Have you got any more information, like when it happened, how it came about that he was playing with several snakes at the same time, and where did he get so many snakes?"

"Doc, they told me they are snake handlers. It's their religion."

The man in the dark coat, wearing glasses interrupted, "The bible says if you're right with the Lord and you got the true faith, you can handle serpents, like it says, and you're safe in the hands of the Lord. You won't get bit. If you do get bit, it means you ain't got the true faith and trust in the Lord, and you are a sinner. The bible is the Holy Word of God, and there ain't no way of gettin' around it."

After his outburst, he folded his arms, thrust out his chest and his chin, and tried to grow taller by rocking up onto his toes, his face alternating between an angry red and the blue from the flashing light of the police car. His righteous eyes glared at me with sanctimonious hatred, then Detective Brown, and swung to the other two men, staring purposefully, sending a message to cower them. His mean, hard eyes fell upon the worried man in overalls and held, fixed there to subdue him. I realized he must be the leader of the cult and the man in overalls was undoubtedly the worried father of the critically ill child.

"You mean to say that they had this child handling poisonous snakes, and that's how he came to be bitten?"

Brown answered, "Yeah, doc. That's exactly what happened. They say it happened at a ceremony a couple of days ago, but haven't told me exactly how many days."

"Great Caesar's ghost, this innocent child is likely dying, because these so-called adults had him holding deadly poisonous snakes." Anger seethed and boiled within me, wanting to erupt and flow all over the three men, but anger must be controlled. If the three men could read my face, there would be no doubt how I felt about them.

Dismissing them from my mind, I turned to Brown. "I don't believe he has much of a chance, they have waited too late. His only chance is to get an IV with cortisone going and transport him immediately to the ER at Eggleston Children's Hospital at Emory University. Get going right now. I'll call my friend, Dr. Patterson, the director at Eggleston's to make arrangements and alert the ER you are on the way."

"Right, Doc."

Drawing Brown aside, I said softly, "Let's get with it, but I don't believe he will make it, Brown. They waited entirely too late before bringing him."

"I know, Doc. It's a damn shame."

The phone call came the next morning. The child did not make it. He died en route to the hospital, his life forfeited by adults in their religious faith, fueled by ignorance, superstition, and fervor in unenlightened minds, and led by a domineering zealot.

Snakes   Case #2: Copperhead

On Easter Sunday the telephone rang during lunchtime, not a favorite time for phones to ring, but seemingly by some twist of fate my meals were inevitably accompanied by the chiding sound of the phone's ding-a-linging message, as if laughing at me by the only means available to it.

"It's the Clayton General Hospital Emergency Room, Doctor Abernathy. We have a patient of yours, a young boy with a snake bite."

"What kind of a snake, and where was he bitten?"

"We don't know what kind of snake, but his father is here and has the snake. He was bitten on the finger."

"I'll be right there, start an IV with Solucortef (cortisone)."

"We already have the IV and cortisone going."

"Great, I'll be there within fifteen minutes, depending on the traffic."

The traffic was favorable. My arrival time was closer to twenty minutes. Inspection of his swollen index finger revealed two tiny punctures where fangs had entered. The little snake was the size of a pencil and measured only six inches, roughly the size of a # 2 pencil. It was a tiny, but poisonous, baby copperhead. I instructed the nurses to inquire at once to the Poison Control Center for the presence of any possible copperhead antivenin.

The copperhead is a relative to the cottonmouth moccasin, both bear living young, usually four to eight at a time. Although this copperhead was small and recently born, it was highly poisonous. The venom of copperhead snakes is poisonous immediately upon birth. Their bite is rarely fatal, except in children.

The boy was eight years old. He and a pal were outside hunting Easter eggs. As he reached into a bush to retrieve a possible egg, he spotted the little snake and picked it up from the ground. As he was moving it from hand to hand, playing with it, the snake bit his finger. Luckily, the boy went directly into his home and reported the incident to his father, who recognized the possible danger. His father tried to "milk" the poison out of his son's finger while bringing him, as well as the snake, immediately to the hospital.

I carefully explained to the lad and his father what must be done. The father agreed and spoke to his son supportively.

"Don't worry, son. Old Doctor Ernie is going to fix it."

Apprehensive, like any child (and most adults), he asked, "What are you going to do? Will it hurt?"

"We're going to play a little game to keep it from hurting you."

"What kind of a game? I don't want a shot."

"You can help me keep it from hurting. You won't even know you had a shot if first we play a game I call "count the ice cubes." I had his interest, but he was still unsure.

"But I don't want a shot." He wanted reassurance.

"I can't promise, but if we play "count the ice cubes", you may not have to have the pain of a shot." A little subterfuge, but a true statement, avoid the pain.

He looked suspicious, but I believed him to be thinking it over.

"Will you count to ten for me?" I asked.

"Why?"

"Each time I touch your finger with an ice cube you count out loud a number, starting with the first ice cube touch as number one. Okay?"

"Where are you going to touch with the ice?"

"At the bite. It is swollen and probably already numb."

"And that's all?"

"That's all you have to do, and nothing will hurt. You know how ice feels? You might feel the first ice cube we count, but maybe not. The tenth number wins the prize, your choice at the Dairy Queen."

The pendulum swung into my favor, when he agreed only to try my scheme. I thought, "I know many adults less brave than this young lad."

The first ice cube was placed and held briefly at the bite site, moving it slowly a few centimeters at a time, back and forth. He said almost immediately, "One." I removed the cube and replaced it with a second cube, holding it a second or two past his "Two." This went on through a sequence of ten numbers. By this time his finger site was numb enough that I was able to clean and sterilize the bite marks, insert Xylocaine, a numbing agent. This permitted me to connect the two fang holes, and open the wound. A suction device was applied to the open wound, attempting to extract venom. After further rinsing and sterilizing, the small wound was left open to drain, antibiotics were begun to coincide with the IV cortisone. Close interval observation was planned to recognize any changes. The nurses were to administer a tetanus booster—after I departed—coward that I was, to let them take the blame for the injection.

The young lad was magnificent throughout, remaining steady calm, although I knew he was just as apprehensive and scared as he had been earlier.

"Why did that snake bite me? I didn't hurt him."

"I don't know, son. The snake was probably scared, being held by something as big as you. That reminds me, you sure have been a big boy while I worked on your finger. When you get home, don't forget you won that trip to the Dairy Queen for you and your dad. I'll go with you and we will have a lot of fun. Get every thing you want, and take some home for your mom. You'll sure have an Easter adventure to tell your friends at school about, won't you?"

That brought a smile to his face. "You are going to be alright now, son." And he was.

SNAKES CASE # 3: UNCERTAIN SPECIES—COTTON-MOUTH MOCCASIN?

Lee Searcy was only about six years old, a bright and cheerful lad who shared times with me in my office, with easy conservation to be so young. He was brought to my office from his home within minutes of a snake bite to his finger. The snake was of unknown type, had apparently not been seen by the parent, but was described by Lee as "little," and the color unsure, but thought probably to be "dark," or "black."

It was possibly a non-poisonous black snake, startled into striking at him, but no chances could be taken since the snake species was unknown. Cotton mouth moccasin snakes have a dark gray to black color, their venom a neurotoxin which causes paralysis of nerves, leading to inability to breathe, and without medical aid can therefore cause death.

As little Lee lay upon my office surgical table, he was naturally frightened, but never moved or attempted to arise. His reaction was to nervously ask, over and over, "What's wrong, Doctor Abernathy?" Scared? Yes, but he never moved. I thought to myself, "What a brave little guy, a regular soldier."

"Don't worry, Lee. The little snake bit your finger, but you and I will get it fixed and you will be alright."

For some reason that now escapes me, I think we did not play my "count the ice cubes" ploy, but proceeded to hurriedly render the standard care as previously outlined in the aforementioned case.

What transcends time and holds a special place for Lee in my memory is his repeatedly asking, throughout the entire procedure as I worked upon the snake bite, "What's wrong, Doctor Abernathy?" (I still recall how he would prolong and drag the syllable "na" in my name) Yet, this scared and nervous little boy held steady as a rock, knowing his friend, the doctor, was there. We shared a critical time together, and we shared a mutual trust.

Lee did well and recovered without consequences. His story is included to show the trust a child and his doctor can develop, and to show the bravery a little boy can possess.

I was not surprised to learn, many years later, that Lee was a Lieutenant in the United States Marine Corps, serving his country with distinction—and bravery.

Snakes   Case # 4: "Snake-in-the-grass"

Case number four is of a different species by which most of us have been bitten at one time or another. That is the species, "snake-in-the-grass." The nomenclature may be only a popular, traditional Southern colloquialism, but they exist throughout the Americas and the rest of the world. For the uninitiated, a "snake-in-the-grass" may be more definitively described as a dirty, sneaking, back-stabbing SOB (as President Harry Truman declared) who cheats his unsuspecting prey, often posing as a friend while scheming to undermine and eviscerate his victim for his own personal gain, be it financial, physical, mental or sexual. Species often include one's best friend making advances on another's mate, as Thelma Viscountess Furness, the married lover of the Prince of Wales, personally found out. Thelma had to leave for a lengthy visit to the United States to testify for her twin sister, Gloria Vanderbilt, at an infamous court battle for custody of her daughter, Little Gloria. Thelma asked Bessie Wallis Simpson, her best friend, to keep an eye on the Prince for her and protect her interest. Instead, Wallis Simpson took over and replaced Thelma as the lover of the Prince, who became the King of England, ultimately giving up his throne to marry twice-divorced Simpson. They became the Duke and Duchess of Windsor.

A used car saleman, stockbroker, business partner, next-door neighbor, or anyone can similarly become a "snake-in-the-grass." The approach and damage caused by one is usually more insidious in onset than other species of snakes, but does considerable destruction comparable to a lesser or greater degree as a poisonous variety. The degree of that harm depends upon the individual circumstance. The wounds caused by a "snake-in-the-grass" leave deeper scarring of their victims, both emotionally and some times physically, to wit—those cases that end in bankruptcy or suicide. There is no available anti-venom, and hydrocortisone will not help. Surgery cannot undo the damage. The result of the bite of a snake-in-the-grass may last a lifetime.

Snakes   Case # 5: A Fable

No collection of snake stories would be complete without a fable. A wise old fox was resting by a stream. A rattlesnake slithered up to the same area, saw the stream and the fox. The snake asked, "Please help me across the stream. I can't swim, but you could let me rest on your back as you cross.

The wise fox replied, "No, I can't trust you. You might bite me."

"Oh, no. I would not bite you. After your kindness taking me across the river, why would I do such a thing?"

"Sorry, I can not trust you," rejoined the wise fox.

"I beg of you to help me across. I will sit on your back quietly. I give you my word, I will not bite you." The snake continued to plead and finally convinced the fox as to his safety.

"Alright, I will accept your word, your vow not to bite me. After all, I will be doing you a big favor. Why should you bite me? Get on my back"

The snake exclaimed, "I am so grateful for your kindness. Thank you so much for helping me." He got upon the back of the fox and they crossed the stream.

The deal having been consummated, they crossed to the other side safely, whereupon the rattlesnake, without so much as a rattle or warning, bit the fox on the back.

"Why did you do that?" cried the fox. "You promised not to bite me, and I brought you across the stream safely."

The snake replied, adroitly, "And you are supposed to be wise? You knew what I was before we crossed the stream."

In this case, the rattlesnake is also a perfect example of a "snake-in-the-grass."

RUMORS

―――•―•―――

"The reason a dog has so many friends, he wags his tail instead of his tongue"

"Dr Abernathy," she began accusingly, "is getting all the boys and girls at Jonesboro Senior High School into drugs. He is getting the girls into prostitution and into white slavery, shipping them out of the country at Port St. Joe, Florida."

The filled sanctuary of the First Baptist Church in Jonesboro, Georgia, was aghast, the pastor staring at the standing "lady" who had interrupted services to make her startling proclamation.

There will be wars and rumors of wars." The biblical saying comes to mind when I recall rumors that flew about our community like a hotbed of swarming locusts. The juicier they were, the faster they flew. The more outrageous and sexier rumors flew at supersonic speed. Central headquarters, and the clearing house for rumors, seemed to always be the local beauty salons, also called "parlors," where little rumors were parlayed into big rumors.

The gossipy rumors were either comedic or sad, sexy, financial, vicious, or scandalous. A few were true, but all were damaging. As a "little fish in a little pond", my own experience being the subject of rumors caused me to pity the "big fish in the big ponds,"—nationally known celebrities, lambasted in the media by many unfounded rumors. Gossip sells, however, and a thirsty public laps it up, like a thirsty dog after a long day's run in a hot field.

False rumors were too frequently spread about me, the physician, in our little community. I was dying of cancer, had a heart attack, was on drugs, had a dreaded terminal disease, or was already dead, (a favorite). I came to almost believe some of the rumors, looking in the mirror each morning to reassure I was still around and kicking. The following few disparate types of my more interesting rumors are worthy as examples.

Rumor One—The Baptist Bombardiers

"Dr Abernathy," she began accusingly, "is getting all the boys and girls at Jonesboro Senior High School into drugs. He is getting the girls into prostitution and into white slavery, shipping them out of the country at Port St. Joe, Florida."

The self-righteous lady, (a patient of mine we shall call Mrs. X), had come to her standing position in the crowded congregation of the First Baptist Church of Jonesboro, a suburban part of Metropolitan Atlanta. A large proportion of the congregation were my patients, as was Mrs. X. The subject under discussion from the pulpit was the damaging influx of drugs in our young population. With a moment of brief delay to insure the complete attention of everyone, the lady, a proud Christian, had begun her own version of a crucifixion.

The gasps that followed her declaration were audible throughout the entire sanctuary. Jaws gaped and eyes stared. The minister stood dumbfounded.

Like a carefully planned, dramatic scenario, a second lady, (another patient of mine whom I shall call Mrs. Y) rose in immediate concert and declared emphatically, "Yes, I know for a fact that is absolutely true." Mrs. Y looked about the room, lips compressed, a barely perceptible nervousness manifest by her rapid, shallow breathing. To add a dash of emphasis, she then looked to Mrs. X and nodded her head rigorously up and down, as if to say, "We did it. We got him just like we wanted." The silence that had pervaded the room evaporated into a buzzing sound of busy voices from multiple small groups, exchanging comments about this juicy and shocking revelation.

The damning was in danger of becoming a chorus, or maybe under the circumstances of locale, a choir—instantly, a third participant, sitting beside Mrs.X. arose. (I call her Mrs. W) She cast her eyes about nervously, looked at Mrs. X several times for support, and finally spoke, timidly affirming in a shaky voice what her Mrs.X had stated. She was obviously intimidated by Mrs. X.

Many of my other patients, present at the time, witnessed the entire distasteful episode. Several wasted no time in informing me, in minute detail, the event as it had unfolded. Others came later to give the news.

How and why did this rumor start? The "how" is Mrs. X and Mrs. Y, ably assisted by Mrs. W. The "why" is more elusive, and like a sordid soap opera, or some kind of elusive mystery shrouded in smoke and mirrors. Certainly, no boy or girl had been reported as missing.

In fact, I was an outspoken critic of drug abuse, giving talks to the high schools, civic clubs and on Atlanta television, as well. The "why" of this vicious rumor was a dizzying puzzle.

Factors that might have led them to such a rabid conclusion had to be considered. Other than vicious malevolent intent, only two other possible explanations came to mind as to how the ladies might have become confused. The first was, in addition to my busy private practice, I did volunteer work with the U.S. Attorney General's office in Atlanta, treating addicts. This necessitated a parade of "weird-looking," scary people (addicts) sharing my reception area with regular patients. The second possibly was my work as County Physician treating the prisoners and addicts at the county jail. Nothing could explain how or why the ladies enlarged their suspicions and fabricated such preposterous conclusions.

At that time, the only place for the formal federal treatment of drug addiction was at the facility of the Federal Prison in Lexington, Kentucky. An addict could not be admitted to the program until a licensed physician had examined them, prepared a typed full report as to their physical condition, and of their addiction. This had to include the full extent of their addiction and of any revealed criminal activities. A letter of referral from the physician was a mandatory requirement.

Robert Smith, the Assistant U.S. Attorney General, asked for my assistance. He stated that he was unable to find any other physicians willing to assist in this requirement, no physician wanted to get involved. Mr. Smith was very persuasive about the need for doctors to get involved and he emphasized his disappointment that the medical community physicians refused to participate. My personal feeling was that treatment of drug addiction was part of the duty of a doctor to his community. After all, addicts are also people in need of medical help. I agreed to give it a try.

The procedure was for Mr. Smith to refer the addicts directly to my office from his office at the Federal Building. I performed the physical examination and prepared the official letter that was required. The subject addict then was to take the definitive letter to Mr. Smith, who promptly transferred them to the medical center at the U.S Prison in Lexington, Kentucky.

To prevent withdrawal manifestations such as seizures, and to preclude further criminal activities such as burglary or robbery in order to support their habit, Mr. Smith had me prescribe a small prescription dose, (usually three to five pills), of the addict's particular narcotic to each examinee. Enough was needed to last through the short time period required between the time of leaving my office until the departure from Smith's office to the prison. The procedure proved effective in avoiding the addict from "coming down" (cold turkey), as well as his (or her) disappearing for a possible relapse to get a "fix." My service was free.

"Doc, is there anything I can get for you, guns, antiques, sex, anything?" (meaning "steal" them for me, thus trying to entrap me). This ploy was offered so many times that I came to expect it, and was surprised if it did not come forth. The addict was trying to favor me with such attentions in an attempt to gain additional doses, which undoubtedly he or she intended to sell, or upon which to "load up" on drugs prior to reaching Mr. Smith's office and leaving for Lexington.

Stealing, burglary and sex were their regular means for obtaining barter materials for drugs, or for cash to buy drugs. A long list of addicts used this scheme, over and over, trying to con me so as to get more than the minimal amount written in their legal, authorized prescriptions.

Physical threats also came from addicts demanding more drugs. They discovered where I lived and would pound on the door all hours of the night. One addict actually lay down on the road blocking my automobile with his body, demanding drugs.

After more than a year in the volunteer physician role with the addicts, I grew weary. When I finally could no longer deal with the personal threats to my family and myself, I telephoned Robert Smith in order to resign. He heaped praise upon me, saying, "We have never had so much success in getting addicts off the street and into Lexington." He thanked me for my participation in that success.

During the approximately one and one-half years I assisted in this program, some pretty unsavory-looking characters had drifted into the waiting room of my office and mingled with my regular patients. This might have been a contributing factor to the outrageous and malignant display of invective displayed in the Baptist Church by those dear, "not-so-little Southern belles." I chose to think of them as the "Southern Belles of Infamy."

The second possible factor was the County Jail. In addition to my private practice, I was appointed the Official Physician for Clayton County, one of the five counties making up Greater Atlanta. For ten years, my duties entailed rendering official opinions, examining all alleged rape cases in our zone of Atlanta, as well as being the acting Police Surgeon physician. The position also included being the medical consultant for the County Jail.

Prisoners in jail who were addicts would demand that I bring into the jail for them the particular narcotic for which they were addicted. Sometimes they threatened me or my family with bodily harm if I did not comply, the injuries to occur after their discharge from prison, or immediately by outside acquaintances they would ask to do the job. "This is a legal institution," I would answer. "I am a legal part of it. What you are demanding is illegal. That is what has brought you to this sorry position in jail in the first place. I am sorry, but I can not and will not do as you insist. I don't want to end up in jail alongside you"

In emergencies, prisoners were also brought through the back entrance to my office, in chains and handcuffs, and seen by patients being escorted in or out of my office in chains and handcuffs. Patients observed the prisoners, and also I might have been seen (in my official capacity) at the police department and about the jail. These observations, combined with the unsavory addict characters parading through my office may have contributed to the darling busybodies expanding their fantasy.

Altogether, duty with the addicts and the jail became a terribly distasteful experience for me. I was relieved when it ended.

Danny

Years later, one of the many addicts that I had gotten into Lexington Prison Treatment Center, (I shall call him Danny), came by my office. He knocked familiarly upon the door to my private entrance at the back of the office building. Danny was impeccably dressed in a nice black suit. He was well-groomed and carried an expensive-looking, black leather briefcase. His face was pock-marked, and he looked much older than his chronological age. He had his usual practiced look of sincerity, accompanied by an equally practiced wide smile which I remembered well. In a soft voice he asked, "Remember me, Doc?"

"Of course, Danny. How are you?""

"Doc, I came to tell you how much I appreciate what you done for me. I am clean (drug-free). You remember all of that bunch I ran with? I am the only one that's still alive, the others went back to drugs and the life. They're all dead except me. I just came by 'cause I wanted to thank you."

"That is wonderful, Danny. I thank you." Frankly surprised, I praised Danny for his personal victory, and I thanked him for the gratitude he was expressing for my limited assistance. I admit I swelled up a bit with self-pride. "Pride goeth before the fall," they say.

After a brief visit, Danny started to leave. He paused at the private exit door, turned to me, informed me he was working at a carnival traveling through the area, and with a very meaningful look said, "Doc, is there anything I can get for you, anything at all?"

Sadly, the implication was quite clear to me. Before he could speak further, I precluded his expected request. I decided to tell an outright lie. I said, "Sorry, Danny. Since I resigned from the treatment program of the Attorney General's office, I don't have a license to write those kinds of drugs any more."

I watched closely to see his reaction, not certain how he might respond. He was silent for what seemed several minutes, staring at me, testing the validity of my statement as best he could. He appeared about to speak, but I elected to head him off.

"No thanks for your offer, Danny, and good luck to you." I stepped in the direction of the door, thus encouraging the conclusion of our meeting.

Slowly, Danny came to a conclusion and accepted the situation. He did not ask for a prescription for drugs, and quietly departed. Through my office window I watched Danny approach an older model pickup truck, where a man was expectantly awaiting him. Danny raised his arms in a gesture of hopeless futility for his friend to see, and shook his head from side to side. His effort to con me had failed. I did not expect Danny to live much longer.

Rumor Number Two—That Blonde Beautician

As my car cruised down the main street in Jonesboro, a lady came running out toward the street, waving her arms frantically in my direction. It was Wilma Shelnutt, a dear lady and friend, who was in charge of the County Family and Children Services Department. She was highly regarded in the region, an important political figure, and was one of my favorite patients. As she neared I could hear her shouting, "Doc! Doc!"

I stopped the car, sure that some medical emergency or tragedy had occurred. "Hi Wilma, what's wrong?"

"Doc, what's this latest rumor I've been hearing about you?"

"I don't know, Wilma. There are wars and rumors of wars. What is the *latest* rumor?" I was sure Mrs. X's unbelievable fabrication about me in the Baptist Church (Rumor Number One) was about to resurface.

She said, "What's this I hear about you and some peroxide-blonde beautician?"

I laughed out loud. "Oh, Wilma, that's not the latest rumor, you are at least six or seven rumors behind the *latest* one. That particular rumor I heard several weeks ago. Since then, I have heard several times that I have cancer. Not only that, Wilma, but I heard only last week, once again, that I had died. As Mark Twain said, 'The rumors of my death have been greatly exaggerated.'"

"Well, Doc, I just wondered, and thought you needed to know." Whether a rumor is true or not, how can telling the victim be conceived as something he needs to know? There is nothing he can do about it.

"Wilma, sweetheart, rumors have placed me in more beds than George Washington is supposed to have slept. I wouldn't have time or energy to practice medicine if the rumors were true, even if half of them were true."

Wilma laughed, "Well, that's so, I guess."

"A Superman, I am not. Casanova, Errol Flynn, and Wilt Chamberlain need not worry, I am no threat to their famed amorous reputations."

Wilma laughed. "You are a super Doc, though. By the way, don't forget you volunteered to do the Head-Start physicals for us on Thursday. Remember?"

"I sure do. And, thanks for the kind words."

"You're welcome. Now, take care of yourself, Doc." She extended her hand, which I took, and gave her a hug.

"Wilma, you are a great friend, and I thank you for your concern." We departed, each to his or her duty for the remainder of the day. I wondered, how many rumors about me had I *not* heard? Especially, about blonde beauticians—for example.

Rumor Number Three—Doctor "H"—A Malignant Rumor

One of the most vicious rumors was the discovery that a gynecologist, (whom I shall call Dr. H), in East Point, Georgia, a neighboring community, had taken upon himself the libelous authority to write a secret letter to the State of Georgia Medical Board. His written words came into my possession by a circuitous, authentic, and covert route. In effect, he stated, that Dr. Abernathy was trading narcotics for sex and guns. I have to assume the poor fool drew his conclusions from the same rumor mill as Mrs. X or some other gossipy, misinformed patient, maybe even from Mrs. X herself, who had perhaps developed a two-pronged plan of attack.

At that particular period of time the State of Georgia had just passed a law that any informer to the Board of Medicine could not be held liable for his statements and sued. If not for that terribly unjust law (repealed much later) preventing my legal action for recourse, Dr. H would have rued the day he decided to play accuser, judge, jury and letter-writer of such fabricated, unsubstantiated charges against me. As it was, considerable self-restraint was also required by me to refrain from punching the little pipsqueak in the nose.

Rumor Number Four—The Beauty Shop

Let's not forget the biggest rumor mill of them all—the so-called beauty shop, or beauty salon, which has become the well-established "American Institute of Gossip."

In any social gathering of men, the subjects most likely to be discussed are sports, hunting or fishing, stock markets, business or politics, often spiced by the additional sharing of off-color jokes with sexual overtones.

Women still flock to the beauty establishments regularly in large numbers, despite the modern ready availability of pre-packaged kits for home care of their beauty, and their hair, by self-administration. Why do they do that when it is more costly, requires more time, and is less convenient? I suspect one reason is because that is where they hear and share all the latest gossip about their friends and neighbors in the community, as well as the flamboyant characters of the entertainment world, a never-ending source of outrageous behavior to discuss.

A beauty salon spawned one of my most hurtful rumors. The instigator was the wife, (now, ex-wife, whom I shall call Mrs. Vicious) of an Hispanic, Cuban surgeon whom I had helped to gain staff privileges in his first private hospital in the United States, Clayton General Hospital (now Southern Regional Hospital of Atlanta). I was the vice-chief at the time, as well as the physician member of the Hospital Authority that built it.

"Dr. Abernathy," Mrs. Vicious said, "had to do emergency surgery last night at the Clayton General Hospital. The surgery was because the woman was bleeding from an abortion he had screwed up, and she nearly died. He and the woman were lovers." (Wonder where she heard that distorted version, if not from her doctor-husband, Dr.Vicious?) Mrs. Vicious did not realize she was defaming me inside a beauty shop owned by my mother-in-law, who overheard the entire episode.

The truth, however, was that the patient was a married, devout Christian lady of the highest morals, a widely respected realtor and community leader, whom I shall call Mrs. Smith. When the rumor reached Mrs. Smith, she was furious and intended to sue both the Hispanic surgeon and his foul-mouthed wife, understandably. Perhaps, she did. I do not know. To be quite candid, I hope so.

I had treated Mrs. Smith and her family for various and sundry minor problems as patients for quite some time. The ER called me one night to say they had a critically ill patient of mine there, bleeding copiously from the vagina, and they suspected internally also. It was Mrs. Smith.

In her attack, Mrs. Vicious had been correct on only one point, the patient did indeed nearly die, waiting in the ER to get into an operating room. I tried desperately to hold her life together with only Dextran (a blood expander) and supportive IV's. The hospital had none of her rare blood type and would not permit her husband with the same blood type to be typed and cross-matched. Instead the Clinical Lab Director, a physician, insisted on sending to Atlanta for blood from the Red Cross, and having the Georgia State Patrol deliver it. This they were telling me, an old combat surgeon? I understood, they were fearful of a legality issue. I was fearful for something more important, the life of Mrs. Smith.

The repair of a finger injury was occupying the surgery suite. It was one A.M. The anesthesia department refused to call in another team in order to open a second operating room, despite being informed of the seriousness of the situation.

By the merest of margins, I managed to hold on and keep Mrs. Smith alive. At surgery, I found a belly full of blood, the source of bleeding was from an enormous ovarian hemorrhagic cyst of endometriosis, adjacent to the fallopian tube junction, which had burst. Control of the bleeding was successful, and the blood pressure stabilized. Post-op blood transfusion from the Red Cross blood was administered, when it finally arrived.

Mrs. Smith survived. She lived to enjoy her family for many years, but some of the people who heard the hurtful lies that Mrs. Vicious was spreading left that beauty salon still believing them, and that thought hurts me to this day.

❋ ❋ ❋

These are but a few typical examples of the myriad of rumors concerning me. Rumors are the natural fodder of people just being people, I suppose, and I should expect more in the future. Hopefully, they will be more of the kind at which I am able to laugh, and not the despicable type of Dr. H. or the hurtful type of Mrs. X, Mrs. Y, and Mrs. Vicious. All of us have had to confront rumors in one form or another at some point in our lives. Some are pleasant to hear, some are humorous, but unfortunately it seems most rumors carry messages that are hurtful. As the news media has demonstrated so ably, bad news is popular.

On a more personal basis, there is an ugly rumor circulating lately that I have been known to watch the entertainment news myself, check out an occasional National Enquirer, or to retell a juicy rumor to others. Likely, just another rumor.

Say, did I happen to mention to you the incredible things going around that I heard about…

A LITTLE GIRL

———•·•———

Abuse

The little body was limp as a rag doll, hanging backwards over her mother's arms. She appeared ashen white and lifeless when first I saw her being carried toward me, down the hallway of my office. Her lips and chin were streaked with obvious recent bright red blood, interspersed with areas of earlier bleeding apparent by the dark blood which was dried upon her face and splattered on her tiny cotton nightgown. It was eleven o'clock in the morning, and she was only three years old.

"Quick, Brenda, get an IV. Gloria, call for an ambulance stat." I hastily placed the tiny, unresponsive, chalk-white figure gingerly on an examining table.

She and her mother were both unknown to me. The child lay pale and ghost-like white upon the examining table, unconscious and unknowing, as life was ebbing out of her. It was readily apparent this was an extreme emergency.

"M'am, how long has this bleeding been going on?" Her mother remained entirely silent and stoically stood beside the examining table watching our frantic efforts to assess the situation and save her child.

"All night," she finally answered. Despite the gravity of the moment, I was struck by the overly calm, seemingly unconcerned attitude of the mother, as though she was having a cup of morning coffee with friends, instead of watching the tragedy of her child dying before her eyes. How do I know for sure this *is* the mother of this child?

"My God, woman. All night? Why are you just now seeking help?: Don't you realize your child has been bleeding to death? She may be dead already? What kind of mother are you?" I let her have it directly, bombarding her with my words. She deserved it.

She made no reply, showed no emotion. Although I was extremely busy with her child, her inappropriate behavior was raising my hackles—and my suspicions.

There was no detectable pulse, no sound of the heart by stethoscope, no visible respiration. She manifest every evidence of being already dead already, but her skin was not yet cold to touch. Nevertheless, every effort in an attempt to save her was being started as quickly as possible, in case there was a chance, no matter how slim that chance might be.

While trying to start intravenous fluids, and supportive medications, I spoke close into the little girl's tiny ear with strong words of encouragement, trying to rally her, although I knew the hopelessness of the situation, and that my encouraging words were probably a lie. I was hoping she might still be able to hear, hoping the spoken words might stimulate a spark somewhere deep in her being and increase her chance to survive. Although her airway was patent, CPR and all our efforts proved to be of no benefit. Sadly, she had arrived in my office too late, as I had feared at first glance. All of our efforts were to no avail, and we lost the battle. She died as I held her in my arms. I was devastated. This poor unfortunate little girl deserved better.

The emergency ambulance arrived to take the body to the hospital about the same time I realized it was too late, she was gone from this earth. She had really never manifest any sign of life since arriving at my office. Her useless death affected me profoundly. Tenderly, I picked up the still form of the little girl and clutched her to me, watery tears in my eyes (tears are flowing again now, as I re-live that event). I held her close to me, certain that she had died from neglect and abuse. "Dear little girl," I whispered to her, "I am so sorry I could not save you." Somewhere deep inside, a little part of me died too.

Turning to her mother, I pleaded, "Ma'am, why in heaven's name didn't you take her to the hospital emergency room last night?"

She did not answer me, the same stony countenance. I continued to stare at her, forcing an answer.

At last, she shrugged and said, "I don't know." To my dismay and horror, the mother added, in a rather casual way, "She was only bleeding like that off and on."

"But, *all night long*?" The incredulous look upon my face was in concert with the dumbfounded repeat of my earlier question, "Great God, woman, why didn't you take her to the hospital emergency room?" My question provoked only the same silence, and a slight shrug upward of her shoulders. She did not reply, or offer any kind of further explanation.

I handed the little girl's lifeless body over to the ambulance crew, but she still lives within my mind and heart to this day.

My index of suspicion was high. There was no question in my mind that the circumstances leading to this child's death needed to be reported and investigated by the authorities. The delay by the mother in seeking obviously needed emergency medical help, and her reticent behavior raised my suspicions even higher to the very real possibility of the child having suffered serious bodily trauma, or perhaps ingesting poisons, etc. Certainly, her neglect had been abusive, to the point of death.

The decision to report it was an easy one for me, but the tragedy of that girl's lost life was not. I reported the case, and my suspicions, immediately the same morning to the authorities for investigation.

Unfortunately, this sad story was made even sadder. My inquiry as to the result of the investigation staggered me. As far as I was able to ascertain, the authorities apparently had not investigated. I reported it for a second time, with the same result. Such cavalier disregard by an authority when notified is criminal, and needs to be accountable. It is equally a form of neglect, and can never be justified. Thankfully, better attention to suspected cases of child abuse has greatly improved in recent years.

Besides this little girl, I recall children of all ages who arrived for care. There were children with as many as 50 direct cigarette burns over some of their tiny bodies, children locked in closets and starved to "discipline" them, children battered and bruised by beatings, children abandoned, deposited on the streets, and children found dead in dumpsters or garbage bags. It saddens and depresses me to think about them once again. As far as I am concerned, no penalty is too great for the animalistic creatures responsible. Let them beware.

❋ ❋ ❋

Newspapers and television news are full of abuse cases, usually after the fact has reached violent levels requiring hospitals and the police to be involved. Non-violent abuse, on the other hand, rarely reach the public domain except in divorce proceedings involving celebrities, but probably account for more cases of abuse than the physical, violent abuse of which we are all made aware regularly by the media. Any individual can be the victim of abuse, be it physical, verbal, loss of freedom by a "control freak," or a domineering misguided parent, relative, friend, even by a complete stranger, ("road rage," where physical violence by a beating or shooting often is the end result.). Have you ever been the victim of "the finger' while driving, thrust at you in traffic by a passing motorist adjacent to you, agitated at you for some real or imagined slight?

It is not only children, wives and girl friends who suffer abuse. Husbands, boyfriends, students and athletes, employees, and many others receive their share also. Boyfriends usually depart, unless they are masochistic by nature. A wife may stay in an abusive marriage "for the sake of the children," as I have been told many times, but her children would benefit more given the opportunity to live and grow in a better environment. Financial considerations may also influence a wife to stay. A husband may remain in an abusive environment rather than face the oppressive financial disaster forced upon men by our divorce laws, whereby they become, symbolically, indentured slaves to the ex-wife, even if the ex-wife is the principal breadwinner in the family.

Such reasons have been given to me many times by patients as to why they persist in an unhealthy, abusive relationship. Our society is becoming more aggressive, abusive, and ready to fight at the slightest hint of an affrontment. Cool it, America.

❋ ❋ ❋

Self-Abuse

Self-abuse takes many forms. It can be purely masochistic, the individual choosing to voluntarily remain with an abusive partner, whether being abused by physical, verbal, or financial means, (for instance, living with as a spendthrift (male or female) who wastefully usurps the family income, leaving the wage-earner penniless, unable to provide for family expenses). The masochistic individual either may enjoy this type of persecution, or relish the repeated proclaiming of his wretched existence—the "Woe is me" syndrome.

Self-abuse may be by physical abuse a person inflicts by injuries to his own body, such as by cigarette burns, knife scratches or actual lacerations, ineffective attempts at suicide that are carefully planned to fail, and by actual suicide and death. Suicide may be an attempt to gain sympathy gone wrong, or a fatal suicide precipitated by a period of depression or despondency as the result of rejection.

Self-abuse physically often is manifest by using the orifices of the body as a receptacle for the insertion of various objects. I have had to remove golf balls, cylindrical tool kits, bananas, coke bottles, dildos, cucumbers, vibrators, everything imaginable from rectums. Lost tampons and foam hair curlers left in the vagina for months were so odorous when removed they would gag a maggot. Other vaginal objects necessary for me to remove included vibrators, a tennis ball, bananas, a ping pong ball, cucumbers, a transistor radio, etc.

One man placed his penis in the end of a vacuum cleaner's smallest extension pipe and turned on the machine, suffering such severe damage that surgery with skin grafting to his penis was required. Another Don Juan experimented by placing his penis in progressively smaller metal rings, known as the "The Nine Rings of Hell," and could not remove the smallest ring, which cut off circulation to his penis. By the time he sought relief, gangrenous changes necessitated the amputation of a significant portion of his penis. His days as a Don Juan were over. William Shakespeare said, "Lord, what fools these mortals be."

Another form of self-abuse is the currently popular masochistic fad of piercing the body with metallic rings, usually silver or stainless steel. Ears, nose, eyebrows, tongue, nipples, "belly-buttons," male and female genitalia, are the most common areas of the body defiled.

Overeating, obesity, alcohol and smoking are considered to be forms of self-abuse, and some critics would include certain tattoos as disfiguring the body, and therefore self-abuse.

Shakespeare certainly knew what he was talking about.

SAVE A SEXIST AND LOSE A PATIENT

Sex. The word has many connotations. It may refer to the beautiful, fulfilling physical and spiritual union of a man and his wife, or merely to the joining of sexual genitalia, whether in a legal or an illegal union such as rape. Sex is the cause of much happiness and also much grief. Regardless of the varied ways sex may occur, it is a driving force for the perpetuation of life, the hormonal machinery that populates the planet.

The experience of life is a great teacher for everyone. This is no less true for a physician, who perhaps comes in contact with a broader range of dramatic encounters with human nature than does the average citizen. In relationships with patients there are occasions that will surprise, shock or sadden the physician, and some will fill him (or her) with a crescendo of joyous gladness. Sex is a cause and a consequence in many cases.

A medical education never ends, but continues in many ways. Of course, formal and didactic teaching in order to keep up to date with advancing medical science is required and scheduled at a myriad of voluntary and involuntary meetings associated with university medical schools.

Overlooked, however, is that medicine in not all science. No medical schooling can adequately prepare a physician for the experience of dealing with people and the interplay of human emotions that will follow, especially with regard to abstracts such as sex, love, hate, greed, death, avarice, hopes, fears, faith, evil and goodness. The physician must "fly by the seat of his pants" as an old aviator saying goes, hoping he is making the right decisions as he continues to broaden and hone his education in human relationships by day to day experiences.

Sex, with all of its ramifications such as hate, jealousy, unfaithfulness, adultery, wife-swapping, guilt, self-abasement, prostitution, disease, and use of drugs accounted for a large part of the emotional problems brought to my office by patients seeking counsel for answers, support, cures, or relief. ("Make the problem go away, Doc") and ("Save my reputation in the community.")

Sometimes it was a simple task, such as medication for a sexually transmitted disease. Other times required the suturing of lacerations, counseling a family, or mending a broken bone and keeping my mouth shut. Just being there and listening to the story unravel was a comfort to some, knowing that someone cared, and trusting in my confidentiality. Unwanted pregnancies, incest, suicide, murder, divorces, rape, same sex problems, HIV "aids" disease, adulterous pregnancies, even bestiality was presented to me. No level of society was spared. The rich, the poor, the well-known, the unknown, pillars of the community, politicians and celebrities, every occupation, the high and the lowly came my way. Each wished for a quick cure and resolution of his or her particular problem and for absolution. Interestingly, many expressed some form of regret for their own actions that caused the problem to arise in the first place, but others remained entirely silent in that regard, their innermost feelings of possible remorse or guilt unspoken.

The medical treatment or therapy needed for the problem presented to me was simply a matter of medical science, well recognized regimens, and was treated expeditiously to the best of my ability. On occasion, I edged into the grayer zones of standard medical acceptance because of an overwhelming empathy for a particular patient's problem and the earnest desire to be of a desperately needed assistance. Science, in its fixation with medical chemical remedies does not take into account the emotional impact and associated stress in these cases, which need attention as well. My pastor might also paraphrase this by saying, "Don't neglect the soul, the spirit."

Towards that end, and regardless of the individual nature of the presenting case, I felt the necessity to offer comfort by counseling using what I termed my "prospective comparative analysis." (PCA, in this age of initializations) First, I hastened to give each individual some kind of solace by pointing out that every one makes mistakes, reminding them in the same breath that in the history of mankind only one person has ever been perfect and never made a mistake. People crucified Him on a cross. We mere mortals will make mistakes. What really counts is how you handle this mistake and how you learn and grow from it to become a stronger and better person, dedicated to a proper life. When and if I could get the wife, husband, or others involved to meet together with me, I made the same statements and tried to show all parties the same sort of common sense wisdom—do you let this destroy your relationship or family and children by dissolution or do you use this mistake to forgive, pull yourself together, and make an even stronger foundation by loyal commitment together for the future. Some did successfully. Some did not.

Throughout the many ensuing years of my practice many of these family situations were observed to remain intact despite the advent of such crises. Vainly, I like to think my amateur "preaching" may have been in some measure helpful in that regard.

Such was not always the case, however. Human nature being what it is, people react various and sundry kinds of ways that seldom follow expectations. Whereas you might anticipate a show of gratitude from the sexist for delivering him from his dilemma, and expect his unswerving loyalty as a patient, often this was not the result. For whatever reason, be it shame, embarrassment, fear, angry spouse or lover, threat to reputation or office, regret of disclosure to me, or for other reasons unknown to me some of these sex-related cases would never grace the confines of my office again after I resolved their crisis for them. Some of these "vanishing acts" had formerly been patients of mine for years.

Gradually, the realization came that a familiar scenario might occur each time I was faced with a new sex-related case. I called the scenario "Save A Sexist, Lose A Patient." All too often it meant losing as patients all of his relatives or family members as well, because of his fear that his relatives might find out about his or her indiscretion. I wonder what elaborate stories had to be invented in order to persuade these relatives not to venture back to me, after years of being my patients. If I could be privy to some of the concocted stories, I would be consumed by either laughter or anger, depending on the nature of the tale. Either way, I bet my ears would burn.

FROM MY FILE OF CASES:

CASE OF MR. X (I SHALL CALL HIM MR. JOHN)—
ONE OF MY EARLIEST "SEXIST CASES"

Mr. John. was an insurance man in his early forties. He and his family had been patients of mine for a number of years. He had telephoned the office and asked to speak directly to me. The dialogue went something like as follows. (and it usually did)

"Doc," he said, "I need to see you in your private office about a very private matter. Can I come over to your office and us talk off the record?"

"Sure, when do you want to come?"

"Soon as possible, how 'bout right after you close today?"

"Give me your phone number, and I'll call you when we finish up."

"Nah, Doc. Don't call me. I'll just come on over when I see your parking lot empty. Can I come in the back door?"

"Sure, I'll leave it unlocked."

That is how it began. Mr. John showed up and looked cautiously about to ensure that he and I were indeed alone in the office. His brow was furrowed with concern and a few beads of perspiration adorned the edge of his receding hairline. It took him several minutes to get up the courage to talk about the purpose of his visit.

Mr. John had been having a sexual affair with his secretary. The lady in question had missed one menstrual period and now was late for a day or so for a second menses. John (Mr. X) was quite distraught, understandably so.

"Doc, this can ruin my family and my business. You gotta help me. I been your patient for years. I don't know where to turn or what to do." He sat on the front edge of an office chair, pulling at his tie and collar, wiping his brow and face with a handkerchief periodically.

I asked the usual questions. Is she usually regular with her periods? Has she skipped periods in the past? Does she take birth control pills or hormones of any kind? Are you certain she is involved only with you? Has she had a pregnancy test done yet? If she had only missed one period, she might not even be pregnant, John. (Trying to give a brief glimmer of hope.)

He knew none of the answers. His agitated state spoke reams to me. I knew his wife and family socially. I understood his anxiety was accelerating and offered the best quick balm I could to ease his distress.

"The only thing I can suggest is this, John. First, I will order a pregnancy test, then…"

He interrupted me to say, "No, Doc, I'm afraid my wife might hear of it. Somebody in the laboratory might know me, or know my wife. Couldn't you do it here in your office yourself?"

"The girls in the office know you, John. Why don't you have the lady bring me a specimen for testing. I might be able to give her a hormone shot to help her start her period while she is here, if she wants me to try it." I was fully aware that an injection was unlikely to make a difference if in fact she was truly pregnant. The effort to show *something* being done however would be of emotional impact and support for him, as well as the lady in question, while we awaited the results of testing, time, and examinations.

"For God's sake, yes, try anything. Please, Doc," he urged.

That is exactly what we did. The lady came to the office, left a specimen, agreed to try the hormone injection and departed. My office staff was none the wiser, so Mr. X's secret was still safe.

A few days later, John telephoned me to say, "Your shot worked, Doc. Thank God. She started." His relief was very evident in the sound of his voice gushing out the words, "Thanks, Doc, I'm mighty grateful." I was pleased for his sake, and for his secretary as well.

I would see John again socially from time to time, but he never returned as a patient to my office again, nor did his family. Unless he or the lady talked to others of their dilemma, we three are the only ones who knew the story. I had "Saved A Sexist and Lost A Patient" (and family) in one of my vividly recalled, earliest such experiences.

Case Of Mrs. X (I Shall Call Her Joan)—
A Highly Placed County Official

It was midday and the staff of my office had left for lunch. Usually, I would have had surgery scheduled during this time of day, but all of the surgery had been completed in the early morning. I was sitting in the office at the back of my clinic building, absorbed in reducing the never-ending pile of paperwork. A series of light, tentative taps upon the back door to my office sounded like someone knocking who was hesitant and unsure of my presence, or themselves.

I opened the door and she was standing there, a dark-haired lady in an elegant dark blue dress suit with a tasteful pearl necklace wearing also a mixture of anxiety, indecision and worry. She and her lawyer husband were well known pillars of the community, and patients of mine. I invited her into my office, informing her that the office staff had departed for lunch and I had no assistants for lab work or examinations.

It took great effort of her to arrive at the reason for her visit. At length, when she finally got up the courage and made the decision to make the plunge, the story began to spill out. This nice lady desperately needed to talk to someone. Something that she had done was driving her crazy with guilt and worry. After considering all avenues, she had decided I was the best bet. Tears streaming down her face, she began to pour out her heart and story to me.

She had blundered into an affair with a very young male, for only a one-time tryst meeting. She was filled with remorse, self disgust, fear for her marriage and her position in the community. She felt she had demeaned the authority of her official office in the county as well. She confided that she had been frightened about the possibility of pregnancy but thankfully that had proven to be an unnecessary worry. Sexually transmitted diseases, (STD), also had to be considered. This lady sorely needed compassion and supportive understanding.

I felt the necessity to offer comfort by counseling using what I termed my homely "comparative analysis," (PCA, remember?), which had become a trusted vehicle by that time. I began by encouraging her not to be dismayed, every one makes mistakes.

"Joan, in the history of mankind only one person has ever been perfect and never made a mistake. He was crucified on a cross. You realize that you made a mistake. You do not need to crucify yourself. What really counts is how you handle this mistake, how you learn and grow from it to become a stronger and better person, dedicated to not repeating the mistake." (Sound familiar?) This lady was in need of compassion and supportive understanding. She had already made her own self-judgment.

Together, we discussed many of the issues, such as whether to reveal her indiscretion to her husband and discuss it with him to reach an understanding, whether to resign her important political position, whether to involve her church's minister, what about the young male in question, and any other issues that we thought might evolve. Pros and cons were evaluated, the issues being "food for thought," to provoke thoughtful consideration on her part in order to reach carefully considered courses of action. Joan never enlightened me as to what decisions she made with regard to any of the issues we discussed, and I did not pry. I reassured her that "this too shall pass" if given time.

Having at last been able to ventilate her story and anxiety to someone, she now calmed down considerably as compared to how she had been when she arrived. Reassurance and emotional support and understanding were what she most needed. These I delivered to the best of my ability with a calm voice, an unperturbed face and demeanor, remaining entirely non-judgmental. For further reassurance, I suggested she might take a broad spectrum antibiotic to allay some of her fear of infection, and a mild tranquilizer to calm her. Samples of these were given to her.

Given a few more minutes, Joan was able to pull herself together, express her appreciation for my help, and she left, no one the wiser for her having been to my office.

The only follow-up I ever had was that she kept her political office and did a great job until she retired. Her marriage endured. Over the next several decades I would encounter her and her husband socially many times and we would talk politely, but I never had the good fortune to see either of them as a patient again. Another "Save a Sexist and Lose a Patient" experience.

Two Cases—Wife-Swapping Parties

The telephone ringing awakened me from a sound sleep. A glance at the clock showed it to be past two o'clock in the wee hours of the morning. The call was from my answering service, relaying an emergency call from a patient whose name was quite familiar to me. He was also an acquaintance and the adult son of a very prominent political figure.

Calling the number I heard his familiar voice say, "Doc, I hated to call you but we got a bad problem here. It's an emergency." He asked me to come to an address not far from where I lived. I knew it was not his home address. I agreed to come, dressed and drove to an unfamiliar two story house by the side of a popular large lake. To my surprise, when I entered the house there were eight people inside, four men and four women, all acting rather mysteriously, glancing guiltily back and forth at each other and rather furtively at me. One woman was sitting in a far corner with a bloody towel held against her face, covering it from my view. I knew two of the men and their wives, recognized a third man but did not know the others.

When I asked what was the emergency problem for which I had been called, they seemed undecided how to respond. No one volunteered. There was an air of hostility and anxiety among the four men and the women that was so thick you could have cut it with a knife. I wondered into what I had ventured. One man's face was swollen and bruised, with caked blood easily apparent about his mouth and nose. The man who had telephoned me spoke up and struggled as to what to say. He began by saying they had been drinking and having a good time, but as it got later things kind of changed, but did not elaborate. Another man, well-known to me, said they had decided to watch some movies. He was interrupted by the first man who explained that things had sort of gotten out of hand and an argument had started. I noticed he was sweating profusely. The smell of alcohol was heavy on the entire crowd. The room reeked of alcohol and smoke, the aroma of the latter suggesting marijuana had been part of the party. He glanced at a tall man with a woman standing beside him, used his hand to wipe his lips, ran his tongue over his lips. He took a deep breath, and added somebody got hurt, as he looked toward the woman in the corner with the towel over her face.

Something was fishy here, but I could not yet figure it out. I walked over to the lady holding the towel and removed it. One side of the towel was soaked with blood. It was the lady's blood from a laceration of her face, on her forehead near her hairline. It would need suturing. Next I examined the man with the bloody face and found another laceration requiring repair. His bruises and contusions would resolve slowly by themselves. When I gave them my conclusions and the bad news, I noticed the crowd began to look anxiously at the man I did not know.

My acquaintance, the telephone caller, said, "We had hoped you would take care of it right here in the house. Couldn't you do that?"

"No." I explained it could not be done there, and that they could have already gone to the hospital emergency room instead of calling me.

That comment stirred up a bee's nest of voices protesting going to an emergency room. The telephone caller asked me, pleadingly, if I couldn't just fix it at my clinic. I began to get the picture, but was still left in the dark about exactly what had transpired. Obviously, they did not want the story to get out. Whether it was the booze, marijuana, or what I wasn't quite sure.

Because of the political ramifications and their worries about notoriety, I agreed to do the surgery at my clinic, using plastic surgery technique to lessen scarring. Six of the eight journeyed to the clinic with me. As I did the work, I noticed they made sure some one of them was present in the room with me at all times. I assumed it was just curiosity on their part, but it could have been to make sure I was not informed of every thing that had been going on at the party.

As I approached the end of surgery, the men all came into the room with the apparent spokesman, the one who had telephoned me. "Now, Doc, I don't know if you are supposed to report this to the police or not, but if you can see your way clear not to report it, we are asking you not to do it. Several careers and families could be ruined."

Our part of Greater Metropolitan Atlanta still had a residual small-town atmosphere and I knew their fears were well justified. Their lives and futures had priority. I told them not to worry and gave instructions for the care of the wounds. They expressed how deeply grateful they were, but none of them ever returned as patients.

A similar incident was to occur almost immediately. It would give me further insight into the nature of exactly what happened that night with the telephone caller and his friends.

A local newspaper article of a second event was my first clue. A nurse in my office brought the rest of the story from a witness she knew personally. It seems that a number of married couples were invited for a party at the home of a physician in our local area. A few drinks had been followed by a light serving of food. More intense drinking of alcoholic beverages was encouraged after dinner. It was announced late in the evening that pornographic movies were now going to be shown in the basement.

One of the men decided to leave with his wife, but she indicated she wanted to stay and see the films. He told her that he was going home anyway, and pretended to leave, but instead hid elsewhere in a closet of the house. He waited there. When he thought an appropriate period of time had passed he returned to the basement scene and found his wife and the physician coupled in a sexually conjugal, compromised position on a couch. The physician's wife was participating with another man in the same manner, and a mixture of other couples were entwined similarly in a busy wife-swapping party. The lawsuit that the husband filed made the local newspaper circulation. Word of mouth gossip traveled faster and farther. The community was abuzz with the red-hot scandal. Divorces and disrupted families followed. The secondary fallout included the unfortunate children, of course.

As the gossip spread, some of the names mentioned were quite familiar to me. I recalled my recent experience when some of those same names had been present the night the lady's face had been lacerated and the man's face and nose beaten badly. I was not completely surprised. My earlier suspicions about that former night were now pretty much confirmed. I had suspected that the "booze and marijuana party" had led to some form of a fighting altercation between participants because a wife-swapping party had deteriorated for some reason into an angry confrontation, resulting in the physical damages I had encountered.

Case Of Miss Y (I Shall Call Her Miss Jane)

One of my regular patients was a family with a daughter named Jane. The parents were owners of a small family business. They were devout Christians and warm-hearted, good people. Their unmarried daughter presented herself in my office because she had made the mistake of venturing into one episode of sex with her boyfriend and now had missed a menstrual period, pregnancy test positive. She was frantic, to the point that she was now nearly dissociating from reality. It was almost impossible to communicate with her. Her language had deteriorated into a form of "word-salad," with rambling and confusing connections of thought and expression. I was able to discern in her thoughts she was entertaining self-destruction in order to escape the situation. She was desperate and not thinking logically. First, I wanted a psychiatrist for her, and consulted her parents, who were shocked at the news but listened to my rhetoric. After calming down, they agreed.

She was taken immediately to a respected psychiatrist. After his examination and interview he phoned to say that, in his opinion he was unsure about her mental recovery unless she could be considered for a legal therapeutically induced miscarriage, or abortion, to recover her mental health and stability. He was therefore referring her immediately to another psychiatrist at Emory University Hospital and School of Medicine for a second opinion.

The second opinion agreed, recommending the procedure. In the state of Georgia, at that time, such a procedure, to be legal, required careful documentation of the findings, the reasoning behind the decision, as well as two certified and notarized recommendations from licensed and respected psychiatrists stating their convictions and reasons for the necessity of an abortive procedure, called a dilatation and curettage. (D & C).

Having fulfilled these requirements, they referred her to a facility for the procedure, with the parents in complete accord with the procedure in order to regain their daughter's mental health, The procedure was carried out successfully.

The return to normalcy by the daughter was striking. Almost immediately, the rambling discourse of "word-salad" ebbed. She eased back into her normal behavior over the next few weeks with the help of medications, but had difficulty with guilt feelings for a longer time. In this case, she and her parents remained loyal patients, and I treated their grandchildren as well. Sadly, however, a confused secretary in my office (for some reason which I never understood) told them something I was supposed to have said about them (not so) and they took exception to it. They never returned to my office again. Loyalty can be a transient commodity.

These cases are merely a few samples of what were repeated many times over the years. People have both pride and shame as well as fears of facing the one who knows their innermost secrets, of which they are embarrassed. They also fear the rebuking recriminations and scorn of their social acquaintances for their mistakes or misdeeds, if the news gets out. The subconscious mind fears that a return to my office might precipitate both concerns—having to face me again and also the nagging worry of running the risk someone else might see them there and somehow might find out.

No amount of persuasion on my part would allay those fears, especially in the ones who felt so strongly the almost paranoid urge for self-preservation. I understood their concerns.

Happily, there were also similar cases that remained loyal patients after favorable dispositions were made in their favor. This group, I observed, learned their lesson well, never making the same mistakes again.

THE VOICE

Moments that inspire us to our best efforts come in various forms, either sneaking into our conscious, unsuspecting presence like the silent footfalls of a kitten in a darkened room, or bursting upon us like a roaring unrestrained rocket of complete surprise. Many such moments came my way while practicing medicine. Some I recognized, and undoubtedly, in an occasional fugue state, I let some slipped away unnoticed. At times, worn out, exhausted and weary, I was in danger of becoming what author Graham Greene first referred to as a "burnt out case." Time and time again, like a preordained gift from some higher power, just when I would be at my lowest ebb, my battery would be "recharged" by some stimulating incident and my commitment resurrected by a fortuitous encounter. These moments saved me and my life's mission, helping people as a doctor. This story is one of those moments.

Unknowingly, a young lad named Wade Scott was to be one of those inspirations. Wade was of average size for his twelve years of age, with dark hair and brownish eye, an aquiline nose, a quick mind, good manners and a pleasant disposition. I had treated him and his parents for a number of minor things over the past few years. His parents were what we call in the South, good people—friendly, blue-collar, "salt of the earth," the backbone-of-America type.

Wade communicated well for his age and the rapport between us was good; we talked easily together about casual things. I was therefore only mildly surprised when he spoke up during an office visit, "Doctor, I know Mom brought me here for my sore throat, but would you take a look at this mole?" He pointed at his lower right leg.

"Sure." I stooped and raised his leg, placing it upon the examining table upon which he sat. Most likely a wart or nevus, I thought. Nothing spectacular or very serious is usually the result, but my first, cursory glance snapped me to full attention. The "mole" was very dark black, only about one-half of a centimeter in diameter. There were suggestions of early irregular margins at the outer edges.

Hoping for the best, I moved in close with an optical instrument that magnified the lesion. My worse fears were realized. Along one edge of the dark lesion an area of inflammation was suspicious as a possible metastasis, or spread. The life of Wade Scott was at hazard.

As softly and calmly as I could, in view of the obvious urgency indicated, he and his mother had to be informed of the probable diagnosis and it's likely seriousness and the need to remove it as soon as possible. I did not want them to feel rushed or pressed in their decision, however

"Mrs. Scott," I asked, "do you know how long this has been present?"

"I didn't know it was there until Wade just showed it to you."

"I don't mean to alarm you, but that has to be removed as soon as possible. I believe it to be what is called a malignant melanoma, a very serious thing."

"What?' his mother asked, uncertain, "that little mole?"

"Yes, ma'am," I assured her. "Don't forget dynamite also comes in little packages, and can cause serious results. This can, too."

"Can we wait until I talk it over with his dad, and maybe do it next week?"

"No, we need to do it right now, here in the office." She almost stepped backward when she heard it was needed so quickly. Expedience was the best course in order to enhance possible prevention of metastatic spread. This was not a case of "haste makes waste," but one of "speed because of need."

"Of course, I may be wrong about the diagnosis, but it would wisest not to take that chance. We should go ahead and remove it, and let the pathology laboratory identify the correct name of the lesion."

The suddenness of this surprisingly bad news was almost more than she could handle, and she was reeling as the wheels in her head were spinning, trying to grasp everything, when Wade spoke from behind me and said quite calmly, "Mama, don't you worry, this is Doctor Abernathy, and he will fix it. I know he will."

Mrs. Scott looked at her son, and smiled, nodding her head, and said "Wade is usually the calmest one in the family, and he says go ahead. I believe it's best, too, so we can be sure." They understood and had made the wise decision to have it widely excised in the office immediately.

The leg was thoroughly scrubbed with the usual preparations and draped with sterile surgical towels. Local field block with anesthetics was completed and the lesion was removed painlessly. The specimen was forwarded to pathology for definitive studies.

As suspected, the report returned with the diagnosis of a "malignant melanoma." The issue of proximal and distant metastasis or spread was raised by the report, and Wade was admitted to the hospital where I carried out exploration of the leg's regional lymph nodes areas up towards the abdomen. Fortunately, all studies of the nodes obtained and other tests performed remained negative for cancer. Wade healed well and went about the business of going to school and growing older, with all periodic reexaminations to rule out recurrence proving to be negative.

A nice story to this point, but my personal inspirational moment came a few years later when this same young lad delivered an envelope to my office, and shyly left it at the reception desk, to be given to me after he departed. The envelope contained a letter of thanks from Wade in his own handwriting. In addition, he had enclosed a poem of his own composition entitled "The Voice."

The document revealed this young boy, with a less than ideal amount of formal education to this point of his young life, had mature feelings beyond his years. The content and flow of his penned words touched me deeply. How he felt and expressed his feelings in his sensitive poetic gesture brought a flow of tears to my eyes. Unknowingly, Wade had come at a needed moment for me; one of those times I was weary, pressured, questioning my commitment to remain in medical practice. From Wade's timely effort, "The Voice," my "battery" received a full charge. Stimulated and re-invigorated, I chose to re-dedicate myself to helping people in what I liked to think of as my personal ministry in the world of medicine.

The Voice—By Wade Scott, Teenager

In thinking back on younger days,
In times of injured fears,
I heard the Voice say, Hey, it's okay,"
To then joke and bring on cheer.

Cancer, the Voice said to me,
With wrinkled face and wrought.
With friendship, faith, and knowledge
The battle was won when fought.

"A marine," I once told the Voice,
"That's what I want to be."
To reach this goal, the Voice
Did all it could do for me.

Some call the Voice, "Doctor."
I call the Voice a friend,
This Voice, comforting voice
That helps me 'til no end.

Surely the hands of the Voice
Are the healing hands of God,
For God did choose to make man
From the dust we know as sod.

Yes, in sickness I came to the Voice,
The Voice told of promises to be,
But cured them all, the kind,
Healing voice of Dr. Abernathy.

✺

I still get teary-eyed each time I read "The Voice."
My eternal thanks for coming when I needed *you*, Wade.

THE COMEDY CORNER

―――•·•―――

JAW-BREAKERS

The office and examination rooms of a physician are usually regarded as a site of serious and solemn contemplation, a gathering center for people with the misfortune of serious physical infirmities and emotional problems, where bad news is received, but it is not without it's comedic, often subtle, lighter moments.

"Doctor," she said hesitantly, "this is embarrassing for me to talk about, but I have to tell you, so maybe I can get something done about it."

The young lady was twenty-seven years of age, an attractive, pleasant school teacher of medium build with ash blonde hair, hazel eyes, a pert nose and an easy smile, but she was clearly troubled.

""I shall be glad to help, if I can," I replied. "What seems to be the problem?"

Probably just another routine medical case really, I thought, having seen how people tend to overreact to minor medical problems in personal, private areas.

She obviously was struggling with the dilemma, to divulge or not to divulge why she was there. A lace handkerchief in her hands was being slowly twisted into knots while she tried to gather her courage.

"Come along," I encouraged, "don't be shy. Whatever it is, it won't be something I have not heard before." Little did I know, being an ever-wise, know-it-all doctor, that I had just stuck my big foot in my big mouth.

"If I tell you, you won't think bad of me, will you? Please, say you won't."

"Of course not, I am here to help you."

"Well, alright, I guess I have to tell somebody, or I can't get it fixed." At last, I thought. She had been standing, now she sank into a chair, afraid her legs might give way as she gathered her nerve. I sat down also, so as not to be in an above position, looking down on her.

"Here goes," she began, "Doctor, I have this problem where my jaw keeps dislocating. It is very uncomfortable and hurts. It is also terribly disconcerting when it happens at the most inappropriate times." She looked at me for a sign of reassurance. "My boy friend hates it when it happens."

"Honey, don't worry, I'm pretty sure we can get that fixed. Any thing in particular or special circumstance that causes it to dislocate? For instance, does your jaw dislocate when you are out in public dining and this upset your boy friend?"

Filled with confidence at the news that her problem could likely be remedied, she released the breath she had been holding, and in a rush said succinctly "Oh, no, it only dislocates when I am giving him oral sex."

Oops! That caught the all-knowing doctor off guard. With considerable difficulty, the urge to show surprise, to laugh or smile was controlled. The young lady was referred to a group of maxillofacial and oral surgeons to undertake the task of reconstructing her jaw, and thusly the resurrection of her sexual prowess, her pleasures—and that of her boyfriend.

THE INTERVIEW

"You must learn to guide the interview when you are trying to obtain the medical history of a patient's illness, and not be distracted by some irrelevant information, stories, or questions, else you are mired down and ineffective as physicians. You must remain in charge."

As early sophomores in medical school at Emory University, we were at Grady Hospital, the teaching facility, listening intently to Doctor Edward Williams, skinny and short, with blond hair and blue eyes, Professor of Physical Diagnosis, our first exposure to actual patient care. This, we realized, was to be real serious advice.

"Now, I am going to bring in a patient to show you exactly what I mean. Pay close attention to how I control the flow of the interview." We were in the presence of a real doctor, and were sure to learn valuable information for our future.

A black man about forty-five to fifty years old was brought in by wheel chair and asked to take a seat in a caneback chair. He had a short black beard along the length of his jawbone, running up to his ear on both sides. His eyes were a dark brown, his nose wide and flat, his teeth were very white against the darkness of his face, and surprisingly his mouth was formed into a very nice smile. He looked very composed. Dr. Williams remained standing. I had the effrontery to think that was a mistake. It gave a feeling as if he was looking down on the patient.

"While holding the patient's chart in his hands, he asked, "What is your name?"

"Hardic Brown."

"How old are you, Mr. Brown?"

"Fifty-one."

"How long have you been a patient at Grady?"

"The Gradies has treated me most all my life, since I was a kid."

"Why are you here presently?

"Cause they said you wanted me here, and they wheeled me down."

"No, no. I meant for what medical reason are they treating you?"

"They looks after my blood pressure, and I got the sugar."

"Sugar diabetes?"

"Yeah, you knows what I mean. I 'speck you know about both them things, don't you?"

"Yes, I do."

"Does you treat people what is got 'em?"

"Of course, but let me ask you…" Dr. Williams was interrupted before he could continue.

"Does the ones you treat ever get well, or just keep taking pills till they die?"

"Well, we usually can control those problems to prolong life, but can't make them go away entirely."

It dawned on me. and I suppose the rest of the class, that Dr. Williams had lost the initiative and was being interviewed himself, no longer the interviewer.

"Don't that mean they never get well?"

"In a way, but the controlling prevents serious complications." The cross-examination was to continue by Mr.Brown.

"Ain't dying serious?"

Frustrated, Dr. Williams snapped, "Of course. Look, let's change the subject," and looking at the class knowingly, added, "Let's get into the past hstory, which may prove helpful. Have you ever had any operations?"

"Yeah."

"What were they for?"

"For? To get me well. They operated on me here at the Gradies two times. You don't do surgery, do you?"'"

"No. Do you know what the operations were for?"

"Sho. Don't you? You got the papers right there in your hands." A sly grin came slipping out.

"I know, but I am asking so that you will tell the young doctors in the room."

"They wuz on my th'oat." He looked at the students. The professor was becoming exasperated.

"What was wrong with your throat?"

"They said it was my tie-rod." A few quiet, muffled snickers coursed among the students.

"You mean thyroid, don't you?" With those words, Dr. Williams had sealed his own doom, never to regain his already tenuous hold on control of the interview.

"No, it was my tie-rod. I axed the doctors and they told me." With that, Mr. Hardic Brown pointed at his throat, looked disgusted, suddenly stood up, walked to the front of the slightly elevated platform, and faced the room of students. His right arm snapped to the horizontal and his pointed index finger swept across the bewildered crowd, his left arm pointing at the ceiling "

"It was my tie-rod, like I said," his words like sledge hammers striking on an anvil. His pointing finger was like a prosecutor in a packed courtroom, sweeping along its path, including everyone it passed into a collective heap, to bend to his will.

"I 'speck some of you in dis room," he boomed out in a strong voice, "done had yo tie-rod operated on. If they is, kindly raise your right hand." He was in his glory when he saw about twenty hands go into the air, accompanied by a light stamping of a considerable portion of the 130 feet of the spectators. His face shone with the victory, and he laughed along with the students, both parties happy, because of different interpretations of the straw vote.

"Let me axe you doctors one t'other thing," Brown began, but Dr. Williams capitulated, threw in the towel, surrendered as a lost cause the intended lesson of the scheduled hour, said quickly, and loudly, "Class dismissed."

Students were hastily leaving, amid the scraping sounds of desks being moved and of their talking together. Mr. Brown, disappointed at the turn of events, was still standing center stage, a lonely figure in a noisy crowd.

The attendant was heading for him with the wheelchair. I walked over to Brown and extended my hand, which he took with a firm grip. "Mr. Brown, I said, "I want to thank you for coming and sharing your medical problems with us. We are just beginning to learn, and you have been very helpful."

His face lit up with his original smile. "I thanks you, young doctor, and I bets you makes a good one, too."

In a different world, with a different background and opportunity, I thought, Mr. Hardic Brown would have done very well, given the chance, and made a real name for himself.

Unusual Names & Words

Some people are stuck with names they have been given at birth, or acquired by marriage, that would make a priest blush. I certainly admire the tenacity, but doubt the wisdom, of people who choose to keep some of these peculiar or shocking names. They have a courage I envy, but do not possess. Perhaps some people enjoy the notoriety of their strange, unusual names, but I would change mine in a New York minute if I were saddled by some of their monikers.

The following are real names of real people. They were both my patients and my friends, nice people, whose names they carried by the fickle finger of fate. I feel they are still my friends, and will not mind or object to the mention of their names, as they have had to use them every day many times, in many places, for many years.

My nurses used to draw straws, trying to avoid being the one to fetch from the waiting area a very nice lady who had, by misfortune and marriage, acquired one of those unlucky last names. The losing nurse in the drawing had the unenviable task of calling the name of the next patient, by stepping to the reception room door, opening it widely, protruding her head through the doorway and into the area, and calling out, for everyone to hear, two short words "Etta Dick."

The same scenario had to be repeated to page a beautiful young girl with a jolly and pleasing personality, whom we all liked, just like Etta. When the nurse looked into the reception area she had to call out "Candy Butts."

Forace

"My baby is real sick dis time, Doctor. He cain't hardly breathe," the mother said worriedly, as she hurriedly placed her tiny pre-kindergarten boy upon the examining table.

The name on his chart was Forace, and I had been his doctor since his birth approximately three years previously. He was the tiny, skinny, young son of a very short Afro-American mother. For his age, Forace had remained abnormally small, causing a sense of sympathetic bonding by me to him. As a consequence of this, he always received special attention each time he visited the office, receiving a gift of a balloon or candy, but I had never seen him this critically ill, and my heart went out to him.

Forace was in severe respiratory distress, the sound of his rasping struggle for each breath filling the room, his skinny little chest straining to suck in air, a frightful condition for anyone, but especially a small tot like him.

Trying to encourage him, I leaned over and softly said, "Don't you worry, little Forace, Doctor Abby is going to make it go away and get you well." Never having spoken his name previously, I pronounced it as "Four Ace," due to my experience with unusual spelling, or misspelling, of names.

His mother swiftly corrected me, exclaiming indignantly, "His name be Forace." (pronounced," Forrest")

Swallowing my embarrassment, and trying not to laugh out loud at the same time, I tried valiantly to hold my professional ""stone" face steady, and proceeded in the task of living up to my words and getting my little friend, Forace, (sic—Forrest) well.

❋ ❋ ❋

Brick Mason, Bright Person, Early Riser, Rocky Stone, Major Miner—real names of real people I knew as patients and friends. Celebrity and historical names were commonly encountered as first and middle names —Marilyn Monroe, several John Waynes, George Washington, Lincoln, Clark Gable and of course Scarlett, Rhett and Tara after all, our town is the home of Tara in "Gone With The Wind") First-name royal titles were given at birth—Lord, King, Princess, Queen, Duke Count, Earl, even "Sir."

One unfortunate newborn was given the first name Wasserman by his illiterate mother, because she liked the name she heard while in the charity hospital giving birth. (at that time, Wasserman was a test for syphilis, a serious venereal disease). Poor child, to carry that moniker through life.

❋ ❋ ❋

Not only the names of people can give us a laugh. The misuse of names of objects can be humorous, and sometimes hilarious, especially when applied to people, intentionally or my mistake.

The patient, a middle-aged housewife of ample girth, was wearing a plain flowered frock of pastel colors and short sleeves, dirty white tennis shoes, and had a tattoo on her arm that said "Steve." Her teeth were yellowed, as were her fingers, from tobacco stains by cigarettes, but she was clean, and smelled of some nice fragrance in which she had indulged herself, undoubtedly in preparation for her visit to my office.

The nurse had already interviewed her and the chart was in my hand, unread as yet, when I asked her, "What can I do for you today, M'aam?"

"Like I told the nurse, the other day I was helping move furniture at the house and got hit pretty hard in the ribs by a chest-of-drawers me and my husband was carrying around when he lost his grip. It is still hurting me to breathe, too." She took a breath and grimaced, to corroborate her claim of pain.

"M'aam, I'll need to check your ribs where you were struck, listen to your lungs and get X-rays to make sure you did not crack a rib."

"Okay,: she grunted, and arose from her chair. To my surprise, she jerked her dress over her head in a flash and stood before me naked except for her panties. "I knew you would need to check it, so I didn't wear no bra," she explained.

Sure enough, along her right rib cage there was a large purplish-blue bruise, already starting to yellow-green. Her lungs were clear. I ordered X-rays.

As she left for her X-rays, I glanced at the nurse's notes in the chart, and laughed out out loud. Nurse Brenda had recorded, in her haste, "hit by Chester Drawers." The entire staff, including Brenda herself, all enjoyed her *faux pas*, the error causing us to laugh so hard we began to cry, as we made our own jokes out of the incident, mostly at the expense of Brenda. A couple of years later a different nurse, Mary Beth, made the same mistake, recording in the chart that a lady had also been hit by a culprit of the same name, "Chester Drawers." This guy Chester really gets around.

※ ※ ※

From time to time, nurses would make other unintentional, laughable entries into the record of patients, sometimes approaching vulgarity by accident. Consider these, which happened often over the years.

Infections occur in many areas of the body, such as tonsils, skin, bladder, etc. Some of these infections may have visible purulent matter present, of which they may be aware and relate as best they can to the nurse, in a matter-of-fact way, "There is pus in the place my son, Johnny, cut on my hand last week," or "Little Mary (or Marty) has a sore throat. I saw pus on her tonsils last night." The mother of the Little Mary would be shocked to read the harried, rushed nurse's note in the chart, "pussy tonsils", meaning "pus on the tonsils," but giving, in fact, an entirely different connotation in the common "language of the street,"—"I did not know tonsils grew there."

Neither did I. In my anatomy instruction at medical school, the possibility of tonsils being located in that particular, obscure, but private, location was never touched upon by the professors, nor found in any of the anatomy textbooks. It was news to me. For sure, I never saw any tonsils during the pelvic exams of my patients.

As to Johnny's chart entry, it was even more laughable, "pussy hand," although the terminology, in common street language, might have been accidentally correct, and understandable, if the particular Johnny was a mid-teen.

Conversely, Little Marty would astound medical science if his tonsils also contained the other descriptive "street" word, (the "P" word), as a normal part of his throat structure. It would be a "first" in the entire history of anatomy. If a "gay" adult male happens to read these words, I suppose he might be amused, thinking allegorically, the combined words in Little Marty's case (the "P" word and the "T" word) could be applied symbolically in his, or his friend's case, with regard to oral sex. The interpretation is in the mind of the beholder, as usual.

Smoke

In medical school in the 1950's, it was not uncommon for medical students to see their professors smoking pipes. Hollywood of the 30's and 40's had encouraged this pose in their movies to affect an air of contemplative wisdom. Many in the real medical community had adopted the style. Medical students naturally wished to emulate certain of their professors, bought a pipe and began to puff away in earnest, and developed their own special poses. Thus started, the habit lasted many years, often into the office of their medical practice. It did in mine.

Mrs. B was full of laughter and wit, a joy to have as a patient, and over the years she became a friend as well. Her adult daughter was also a regular patient. Both had curly blonde hair, blue eyes sparkling with humor. Mrs B was a lovely lady whose beauty was matched by her lively personality. She was the antithesis, the exact opposite, of the "dumb blonde" as portrayed in jokes and movies. She was intelligent, witty, vivacious and as ready to discuss Dostevesky as easily as the Three Stooges.

One day, to my everlasting chagrin, using her own knack for humor in my office, she taught me an enduring lesson that changed my life. In those days I was still smoking my pipe, as usual, and absent-mindedly walked along with my nurse into the examining room, where Mrs. B was upon the examining table, prepared for a pelvic exam, and a pap smear. Mrs. B and I chatted about this and that in our usual pleasant, bantering way. As a matter of routine, and without thinking, I sat down upon the positioned office stool as we talked, my pipe still in my mouth, with smoke now wafting upward between her shrouded knees in the stirrups. As she lay covered upon the table, the smoke drifted on it's way toward the ceiling and came into her field of vision.

Mrs. B noticed the wisps of smoke arising and, quick as a wink, she laughed out loud and inquired, "Good heavens, Doctor Abby, am I on fire?"

My shock and embarrassment transfixed me, speechless. Mrs.B, kind lady that she was, helped me out by saying, "That's the best laugh I have had in a long time, Doc." I apologized profusely, but between outbursts of laughing, she insisted, "Don't worry about it, it's not a big deal, but what a chance for me to toss out a great line worthy of Henny Youngman."

You can safely bet that was the last time I ever smoked a pipe in my office. In addition the incident was an elemental part of my ultimate decision to give up the smoking of a pipe completely, after more than twenty years of previous use. I was fortunate that my *faux pas* was with Mrs. B and not some less tolerant individual. Together, Mrs.B and I laughed about that incident for years to come. I still do, but you can bet I am filled with chagrin each and every time I recall the circumstance. It's good, I guess, that I cannot go back and change the outcome, it would mean the loss of a great many moments of shared laughter that was generated as a consequence.

In our present day environment of concern about heath problems related to smoking, it probably seems incongruous for a doctor to have been smoking in a medical office, but in that earlier era of the sixties it was a common enough occurrence.

✽ ✽ ✽

Pride And Joy-Juice

"Doc," Coach Bud Amsler said with exasperation, "our guys just don't have enough pride, you know. That's the main thing. I keep telling 'em, if you have enough pride you can win."

It was best, I thought, not to comment that his high school team had just lost their twenty-ninth consecutive game. in a row. That kind of record is not conducive to building a great deal of pride.

Bud was a deep-chested, square-jawed, pleasant man of medium height and build with a ready smile, an easy laugh. He was a teacher who had undertaken the task of being the football coach at Jonesboro High School. He looked like a football coach. I was the volunteer doctor who did the physicals, treated injuries at practice or at games, which I attended by sitting with the team on the field. It was the mid-1960's.

"Pride, pride, pride," Bud said. I've been drilling that into them for years now, and they just don't have enough pride. That's why we lose."

It would have been helpful if they had been instructed and drilled more about how to tackle, block and execute plays, I mused, because I had observed the team on the field.

Pride? During the last game, a fleet halfback with natural talent but no helpful or definitive instruction, had made an excellent return of a punt, gaining half the length of the field. At the end of the play, he calmly trotted over to the sideline, not to where the team stood, but farther down the sideline where, to my surprise, his parents were standing, instead of being in the stadium seats. I watched him talking animatedly with them, as he reached into a large bag of buttered popcorn his mother was holding. He helped himself to a few handfuls, and resumed discussing his exciting play.

I had to laugh at the comical scene of a player gulping down popcorn, unconcerned about being with his team and coach. Pride? Besides instruction, what they also needed was discipline. No coach I ever knew, or heard of, would have tolerated the parents being on the playing field, the popcorn, or the halfback not returning to the team.

"And those dad-blamed leg cramps don't help," Amsler added. "The main thing besides lack of pride is the guys are not in shape, that's why they get the leg cramps. Do you know how much time we lose players out of the game because of leg cramps? It's plenty."

"I've been thinking about that, Bud. I have an idea how I might be able to help prevent the cramping."

"I wish you could, Doc."

"I'll work on my idea and let you know. Maybe, by the next game, I'll have something ready to help."

Loss of fluids and hydration and changes in chemicals called electrolytes, such as potassium or sodium, I figured, played a major role in causing the muscles cramping in the legs of the players. If I could stop the cramping or lessen them, it would be helpful. Realizing this led me to an idea worth trying in the next game.

The game was going along fine, except we were losing—again. It was nearly time for the halftime intermission. The star defensive tackle, a big over-sized teenager with real talent, was beginning to have leg cramps and was removed from the game.

In the locker room, my experiment was about to unfold. "Coach," I said, drawing him aside. "I have made a solution that may be helpful with these leg cramps, if you want to try it."

"What is it?"

"It's made up of water, glucose (sugar), and some chemicals, like potassium and sodium for example, that players have trouble with when they sweat. Leg cramps are caused by these chemicals changing when you sweat profusely while exercising. I believe this concoction will help." I showed him small medicinal paper cups used for pills or small medical doses at my office. "We could try small doses of this size first." Not a scientific study, but practical and timely anyway, I thought.

"Anything that might help would be a godsend." He turned toward the team.

"Listen up, you guys," he directed. "Doc has a drink here that may help stop the leg cramps. He has these tiny paper cups, one for each of you. Sip it slowly, but finish the cupful."

"What's in it?" several cried out.

"Never mind. Drink it." Never one to waste time explaining, he gave the order.

As far as I could tell, most of them did. I noticed the star tackle was taking an extra two cupfuls before I could object. His reasoning, I guess, was if one was good, three must be that much better.

The best plans of mice or men, as the saying goes.

Several of the players began to throw up (vomit) the purplish liquid and the star tackle was retching uncontrollably as the half-time intermission ended. Those players who were able, headed for the playing field. I remained behind amidst another type of playing field—players in various stages of either nausea, vomiting, or retching with dry heaves, the star tackle the worst of the entire lot. I was standing among a roomful of nice young men I called friends as they were in various stages of regurgitating their brains out, and I was the dirty rat who made them sick instead of helping. It had seemed like a good idea at the time, but the result was disastrous. Like the "wave" made by fans at a sports event, the players were making their own multiple frenetic wave, bobbing up and down as if in some macabre dance to new age music.

I was filled with remorse at being the cause of their discomfort, but puzzled at the same time. Why had the fluid prompted this kind of reaction? It should have worked. Had my test mixture been too concentrated? Perhaps I needed to add some flavoring. Although I still believed this would be the answer to solving the leg cramps problem, I resolved to try no more experiments, knowing the players would undoubtedly refuse to participate. I was just hoping they would not start calling me, "Doctor Vomit."

The players in the best condition trooped back onto the field for the start of the third quarter. Players who were more affected and sicker were able to venture out of the dressing room to the field early in the third quarter, however, it took longer for the big tackle. He arrived near the end of the third quarter, but was so weak he could not yet resume play.

The outcome of the game was not affected by my experiment, as the team was already far behind at halftime. The star tackle went on to play tackle for Georgia Tech, and became a closer friend after his playing days were over. Bud Amsler moved on to a school in a new territory to coach. The team began to win games. I continued the practice of medicine and left the experimenting to others.

My experimental solution was a good idea, and I should have continued investigating it, adjusting the ingredients until it was better balanced and therefore effective. Some one else did, a little later. Ever hear of Gatorade?

❋ ❋ ❋

S.O.B. Or Not To Be

The doctor sat in the witness box, a chart in his hands wherein was written, in his own handwriting, "The PT came to the ER in CHF with SOB and DOE." Translation: The patient came to the emergency room in congestive heart failure with shortness of breath and dyspnea on exertion—(made worse by exertion). Translation by a litigation lawyer, sneering: "Doctor, your jargon is not specific. It is possible that your note could be interpreted to mean a form of boat called a PT crashed into an exercise room while in a cab or carrier with a sun-of-a-bitch and a deer." Members of the jury smiled, giggled, or looked angry. The spectacle of the doctor's destruction was just beginning, hastened by his own lack of alacrity and his constant use of acronyms and initials instead of words throughout the medical record, a very costly mistake.

In medical school, professors decried the use of initials and acronyms, insisting, "Your patient may see your notes and resent being referred to as an SOB, for instance, not knowing you mean shortness of breath, and his lawyer will use it against you. You use PND, for example, to mean "post nasal drip," but also use PND to mean "paroxysmal nocturnal dyspnea", (intermittent shortness of breath during the night). How is one to know exactly what you are intending to say? Confusion reigns. You are to never use initials or acronyms."

Then came military service, where no possible use of initials or acronyms was allowed to go unused. The idea infiltrated into civilian life. Every Tom, Dick, and Harry (TDH) makes up ASAP his own acronyms, (HOA), or initials. By exponential extrapolation, we could eventually have over three-hundred million individual acronymic languages in America, debasing the English language altogether. In that event, I fear we would sound much like the Cro-Magnon man, grunting mono-syllabic utterings, indecipherable to the intended recipient, who has his own equally-indecipherable acronymic language of grunts.

In today's world, acronym usage is commonplace, and we take it for granted—*if* we understand the intended meaning. If unsure, the tendency is to ignore the acronym and live in ignorance as to the importance of what it may signify, rather than risk the embarrassment of having to ask someone and seem not to be "with it," or "cool," as the kids say today.

The UIO (use of initials) in our society (IOS) has eroded the UOW (use of words), PDQ (pretty d---n quick), to COM, (convey our meaning), and it is regrettable, (IIR). Think how many such examples of acronyms or initials that you run into daily in newspapers, television, and in normal everyday language, such as FBI, CIA, UPS, COD, IHOP, UNICEF, NASA, UN, NRA, and the list goes on ad infinitum. Initials have permeated our language. They are here to stay.

UIO IOS HET UOW PDQ COM, IIR. SWIM? (See What I Mean?)

❋   ❋   ❋

A Short Note On Deep South Southernese

Although born and raised in four states in the so-called Deep South, my home at various times was in the east, west, north and the South of this great country. Notice the Capital "S" in South? (Feel free to capitalize the first letter of your own region, if you have pride in it—and I hope you do.)

Every region has an accent, sometimes many accents, a collection of idiomatic expressions peculiar to that region, as well as unique colloquialisms. Some places are notable for a "lack of accent."

For the latter label, "lack of an accent," the South, New York, New Jersey, Massachusetts, and New Hampshire and a few others need not apply. The South, in particular, is disparaged unmercifully. Now, ya'll cain't deny it, gotta admit I'm rite." Now, ya heah?

On occasion, Southern "English" is tough enough for natural-born southerners to easily comprehend. We slur and drag out certain words, lazily join others together, saving energy and time, and use words that only sound like the words intended. (See the last short paragraph of this section.)

This puts you other folks in a "pickle trying to figger out jes whut we mean." Others have penned more extended and complete Southern vocabulary volumes. Here are a few sometimes omitted. Test your self.

Pain in my "grind"—something hurts in the area of the groin, or "privates."

Problem with my "nature"—something is not going right with me sexually, which includes all kinds of possibilities too numerous to list. Possibilities include every thing known to impede, or affect in some way, sexual performance. Use your imagination.

I took some Yellow Root—a nonspecific southern root, yellow, used indigenously as a "cure-all" for everything, saving use of a doctor as a last resort. The root has been reported to contain significant amount of acetysalycylic acid, (simple aspirin).

We ate some "Poke salad":—a wild growing weed, non-cultivated, easily found in the South, cooked similarly to turnip greens, collards, somewhat like spinach, but of no proven nutritional value of which I an aware.

Sassafras tea—the sassafras (saxifragia-SP) tree is a branch of the laurel family, the bark of its root yields an aromatic stimulant. It is used also in cosmetics.

Pot Likker—No, it is not the flapping of a tongue on a big fat belly; it is the residual juice left after boiling turnip greens, popular drink in the South, but not for this Southerner

A few others: wadn't (wasn't), idn't (isn't), fixin' to do something, (about to), crank a car (start it), and winder (window).

Now, y'all come back to see us, ya heah?

KITCHENER

Some innate, primeval feeling of danger crept into my deep sleep, and I knew fear. Slowly opening my eyes, I could make out a dark form silhouetted in the moonlight, and two luminous eyes staring fixedly at me less than eight inches from my face as I lay in a sleeping bag in a cow pasture outside Santo Domingo. The 82nd Airborne was there by order of President Lyndon Johnson to quell a revolution incited by Che Guervera, who had come from Cuba for the purpose of leading it.

"Come on, get up, let's have a knife fight." The voice came out of the shadowy dark form. Oh, no. It had to be Kitchener—again.

Indeed, it was Corporal Kitchener, a recent addition to our MASH unit, the 15th Field Hospital. He was making another of his quiet stalks of me in the wee hours of the night. For some unfathomable reason he had picked me out as his prey.

"Go away, Kitchener. I told you, I'm not going to do that."

Kitchener was a near-illiterate man of small stature, about thirty years of age, with a solid body, a face scarred by acne, a bent nose from some previous trauma, blond hair, and a fluctuating disposition; from stormy to sunny, and vice versa. I was aware of his history. He had been a Ranger in Korea, where he was dishonorably discharged for killing an entire Korean family who had reported him for stealing one of their chickens. Five murders, for one chicken. He joined the Navy next, with a similar result, dismissed for similar serious charges. He was a killer. By some means, undoubtedly devious, he had managed to enter the Army again.

"Come on," he urged, "let's have a knife fight, just you and me, to the death." The maniacal gleam in his staring eyes was no less disconcerting than the rhythmic gnashing of his teeth and clinching of his mouth.

"I'm tired, man. Go way, I'm trying to sleep." It had been hectic the previous day, with multiple casualties needing surgery into the night, and I was exhausted.

Kitchener continued to squat beside my supine position. He was capable of thrusting a knife blade into me as I lay there defenseless, I knew, so distracting him seemed a good idea. "Say, aren't you from Indiana?"

"Yeah, how'd you know?"

"Your 201 file, I think, or somebody told me. Where in Indiana?"

"Near Richmond, on a farm."

"My first wife was from near there, Greensfork, Indiana."

"I know where that is. It ain't a very big place."

"Look, Kitchener, we had a lot of surgery yesterday. I really am tired and need to sleep. Go get some sleep yourself. Okay?"

To my relief, he answered, "Yeah, okay, if you ain't gonna have no knife fight with me." He slipped away into the black of night, as quietly as he had come, like some illusive shadow that you were not sure was really there at all after it disappeared.

I lay awake wondering why he had chosen me to challenge for something as serious as a knife fight. Was it because I was the chief of surgery and wielded a knife myself, a scalpel? Was it the "little-man" Napoleon complex, because I was six feet, three inches tall, and he was so short? Or some other unknown reason which I could not figure out?

The next day was relatively quiet, with little action. From around the corner of the surgical tent where we were checking equipment, Kitchener strolled into view and said, "I've got something for you." He stepped very close, bringing me to full alert.

His right hand came from behind with a swift movement and thrust at me with vigor. My eye caught a shiny flash from the end of the sharp object, as he shoved it at me, the belly muscles tightening and preparing for a blow I could not defend. The point jerked to a stop just before it struck my waist.

A big, malicious grin was on his face, at the success of his subterfuge. To my surprise, the object was a gift he had made for me, a "swagger stick," similar to those as carried by British officers. Kitchener had divided a 50 caliber machine bullet in half, put the polished and shiny front half on one end of a round length of highly polished and waxed wood, nearly two feet long, and the remaining half at the other end. It was a beautifully crafted piece of work, for which I was extremely grateful, and told him so. Somewhere deep inside Kitchener it seemed there was a redeeming feature wanting to surface, to be let out. Meanwhile, his waxing and waning, aggressive behavior and schizoid personality persisted, leaving me a "nervous Nellie," especially while trying to sleep.

Surgery was being performed in a cow pasture tent, often standing beneath poor lighting in ankle-deep rain water during the rainy season, with the occasional sniper attack to remind us of serious and unpleasant intentions. Many weeks later, we had actual rooms in a building which we "liberated" from the Dominican Coast Guard/Naval Academy, just across the Duarte River guerilla headquarters of Che Guervera. Surgeon General Heath in Washington purportedly remarked, "It is the first time to my knowledge that casualties have had to be evacuated to the front for medical care."

In the new environment, with an actual roof over our heads, hospital headquarters discovered the carpenter and handyman skills of Kitchener and he was now around daily. He had found himself a niche and "safe harbor," working for hospital headquarters office. Consequently, he seemed calmer, to my relief. No more challenges for knife fights, and I slept easier—but with "one eye open," just in case.

In our combat area, there were cycles of intense activity and occasional periods of boring tedium, especially at night, waiting for what tomorrow might bring. When all else failed, inventive ideas often were the means of relief from the boredom of inactivity, and the chronic build-up of tension.

One night, for comic relief, we applied a wild suggestion of Captain Bill Goodson, the 82nd Airborne psychiatrist on the hospital staff. His idea was crude to the extreme; understandably; only a psychiatrist would have come up with it. Each of us in our little group was to write down on paper one complete sentence, to contain the most crude, vulgar and profane words known, then we drew straws to see who had to sort and read them in the form of a story. The doctor group included Captain Billy Wolfe, Captain Walker "Dub" McGraw, Captain Sebastian "Sibby" Fasanello, (former child prodigy concert pianist), oral surgeon Major Ed Strong, Captain Tom Cochran, Goodson and myself. As the reading progressed, we laughed until we cried, tears streaming. For some reason, Kitchener came to mind; how thin the veneer actually was between us and him, I thought, considering what we had just done. There is no denying the childish and inane nature of what we had been doing, but it worked, the embarrassing and tension-relieving guffaws were successful in bringing us out of the mixed doldrums of boredom and chronic tension. Goodson knew what he was doing.

Fortunately, our parents, wives and relatives back home were spared knowing how irreverent and ill-considered we had acted—unless they read this account, and can fathom the pressure we were under as the few doctors there at the time for the 28,000 combat troops.

In a similar state of minds some weeks later, my anthology book of poetry caught the eye of Captain Billy Wolfe, hometown Savannah, Georgia. Wolfe suggested, "How about us taking turns reading a few selections of poetry out of Ab's book?" A few heads turned. "We could take turns reading out loud."

"Billy, I don't think this group is into poetry much," I countered. A mild chorus of protests rose to disclaim my opinion, the result was we would undertake a trial run to "test the water."

Our little group this night was made up of the doctors and some of the enlisted men who worked with us, like Fred Lewis, and Larry Snow. Kitchener dropped in as Wolfe was reading Poe's "Ullalume." I was surprised Kitchemer remained until we finished reading for the evening. Longfellow, Edward Arlington Robinson, Poe, Algernon Charles Swinbourne, Whitman, Frost and others were read for all to hear. Although the scene might be thought bizarre occurring in a combat area, combat itself is bizarre.

A few nights later, the opportunity presented itself again. We were sitting or reclining on our army folding, wooden cots, in various states of undress, fatigued after a busy day, and receptive to the idea of escape. The poetry anthology was retrieved.

"Read that one 'bout that bird," Kitchener shouted above the cacophony of voices calling out their individual requests, like a bunch of kids in a candy shop wanting everything at once. Somebody yelled, "We haven't heard from Sandburg, read a Carl Sandburg." The book was in my hand, it was my turn to read, and this child wanted Swinbourne.

The tattered anthology book with the loose cover was opened, and we were debating between Swinbourne and Sandburg. Meanwhile, Kichener loudly persisted, over and over, "Read that one 'bout that bird."

Finally, it dawned upon us, to our collective surprise, that it was Kitchener who was trying to get our attention. Kitchener had been a silent spectator in our little reading group, but no one expected him to have an opinion. We were caught off guard, shocked. Some one in the crowd asked, "What did you say, Kitchener?"

"You know, that bird what don't give a shit." A round of chuckles and laughter followed his expressive terminology. Who were we to be critical, after our own crudeness of expressions on "Bill Goodson" night?

Sibby asked, "What are you talking about, Kitchener?"

"That bird, the one what don't give a shit," he repeated, unable to express himself in a less odorous fashion.

Wolfe suddenly saw the light, and exclaimed, "Oh, I believe he's talking about Poe's "The Raven." Kitchener, is that it, the bird that would only say 'Nevermore' as his answer?"

"Yeah, that's it, the one where the bird didn't give a shit! I like that bird." He grinned, pleased at showing he remembered the poem, and eager at the prospect he was gong to get his request granted.

The conversion of Kitchener was so dramatic, Swinbourne would have to wait. I turned to "The Raven," and began to read. Kitchener deserved it, for having shown his awakening to the strength of poetry, regardless of his expressive interpretation. As I was reading, a beatific glow of satisfaction spread upon the craggy face of Kitchener. His eyes closed, his head tilted backward, a wide smile stretched his closed mouth, as if to say, 'I told you so," The former laughter at Kitchener's voiced impression of "The Raven," wound down to a quietness in the room, as if the others recognized for the first time some new quality in Kitchener which they could not yet comprehend.

"See," he said, as the reading finished, "like I told you, that bird just don't give a shit."

The scene was comical in a way, but very touching to see his awakening to poetry. Paintings are said to be interpreted differently in the eye of different beholders. In his own vernacular way, Kitchener is proof the same holds true for poetry; whether the encounter of discovery is by visual, ritten words or by auditory means.

One day, Kitchener, came running around the corner of the aid station, excited, shouting, "Doc. They're lookin' ever-where for you. Want you down to the pad right now. A chopper is coming in emergency, just to get you. Something happened to the general. Reckon he got shot?"

Sure enough, the rotors "whup-whup-whup: could be heard getting closer by the second. It must be something mighty bad, I thought, to be sending an emergency chopper for a surgeon.

General Bruce Palmer, three star general, was the commanding general of the 28,000 troops. I had never laid eyes on him. How could he be sending for me by name? The C.O. of the hospital, an orthopedic surgeon, must have recommended me, instead of going himself. That must mean, I thought, it has to be a serious surgical emergency, a terrible injury, maybe a sniper got him, or a grenade thrown into the passing vehicle of the General.

"Ours is not to question why, but to do or die," as the saying goes, so no more precious time was delayed wondering, but used more efficiently to grab the all-purpose surgical kit being thrust at me by a nurse anesthetist, and to hustle down to the launching pad where the crew of the chopper was anxiously awaiting the arrival of some important V.I.P army surgeon, not knowing it was just plain old me.

"Get in fast, Doc. General Palmer needs you real quick," the crew chief announced as he pulled me into the aircraft and gave a thumbs up sign to the pilot. The engine revved up and we launched into the sky, heading to whatever the crisis was that had befallen General Palmer, the nature of which no one had told me. Boy, I thought, I better be on my toes with this one, to lose a general would mark me, or any other surgeon, for the rest of his career in the army, or on the outside in civilian life. Not knowing what to expect was the hardest part of waiting.

The chopper landed safely and I was greeted by a Lieutenant Colonel and a Major who were very tense and nervous as they grabbed my arm, hurrying me from the landing toward an adjacent building I presumed to be the grand headquarters of our illustrious army. Their anxious attitude confirmed my suspicion that the general was in a bad way, his life ebbing away, in danger of losing his life from whatever calamity had happened to him.

The officers guiding me were joined by an Aide-de-Camp of the General and we all rushed through a doorway into a large room which contained a huge desk, behind which a man in military uniform stood, facing the opposite way. I wondered if he was lamenting the loss of his general. I scanned the room quickly for signs of blood or trauma, expecting to see a prone bloody body on the floor somewhere.

Just as I realized my search was fruitless, the man behind the desk turned and he was wearing three stars. He was General Bruce Palmer, a short, thin, and wiry man, "god" as far as his soldiers were concerned. His uniform was immaculate, no blood, no signs of trauma. All I could do was wonder what I was doing there, and what was the big emergency that brought me there, and to salute, saying, "Captain Abernathy, sir. How may I be of assistance?"

"Captain, If you can stop my diarrhea and cramping I would be grateful."

That's it? Emergency helicopters, surgeons, panic in the streets and in the headquarters staff because of diarrhea? No trauma, spurting blood, gaping wound, no general on the threshold of dying in combat, his life slipping away and the valiant surgeon challenging that destiny, saving the general in the nick of time? I wanted to burst out laughing, but liking to believe I am not entirely a fool, I kept a straight face and treated the general for diarrhea. It turned out that General Palmer, later to have command in Viet Nam, was a class act, a gentleman. He thanked me for coming to his aid.

I was then promptly shown the door by his aides, and ignominiously returned to the hospital, not by helicopter, now that the "shootin' was over," but by riding in a lowly jeep, through guerilla territory via the only corridor kept open by the marines.

Seeing my arrival, Kitchener rushed over, "How bad was his wounds? Did he make it? What happened?" He couldn't wait to hear all the gory details, but that was Kitchener, he had a fondness for gory details.

"Kitchener, old scout," I toyed with him, "It was terrible, one of the goriest scenes I ever saw."

"I don't see no blood on you." Kitchener, ever the observant, where horror, mayhem, murder and maiming might be a factor, was correct.

"Being a general," I explained, "he might get a new authorized combat ribbon for his uniform, but it will have to be brown."

"What do you mean?"

"The general's big combat emergency turned out to be diarrhea."

"Shit," he said disgustedly. In his vernacular zone, Kitchener had a way with words.

"Exactly." No one, erudite and articulate, could have summed it up any better.

Sadly, Kitchener ended up being shipped back to the States in a strait jacket, the only means that were available to subdue him in another of his murderous, agitated mental states. I never learned the details as to what he might have done to precipitate his confinement, because I was transferred back to the States about that time. Knowing Kitchener as I did, it could have been anything, including the knife fight he was always seeking.

BOB HOPE

"Bob Hope is coming!" The word spread like a raging wildfire throughout the 82nd Airborne troops in the combat area of Santo Domingo, Dominican Republic. Despite fighting to suppress the revolution, excitement reached a feverish high pitch, especially among the many wounded where they lay in improvised beds made from olive green folding cots resting in row after row in the 15th Field Hospital, finally quartered in an actual building with a solid roof over their heads. No more tents.

The surgical unit previously had been encamped in a water-logged cow pasture adjacent to downtown Santo Domingo and the Duarte River Bridge. Reportedly, as a result of the early guerilla uprising, an estimated four to five thousand rotting Dominican bodies had been sprayed with lime by the World Health Organization and bull-dozed into the river as a mass grave. We had been trying to save soldier's torn and shot-up bodies, operating upon them where they lay on stretchers placed upon carpenter's saw horses, in canvas tents, sometimes under the light of a single hanging light bulb, often while standing in ankle-deep water, the occasional round of a bullet coursing through our compound and surgical tents. From sleeping bags on the ground, shared with tarantulas, we progressed to sleeping bags on folding cots still shared with tarantulas. Sniper fire from a nearby building passed just over my own head in that original "mudville" locale, when I had been stupid enough to stand alone atop an elevated rise in a clearing within range.

Our new location was in buildings formerly of the Dominican Coast Guard Academy facility, by the side of the Duarte River, just across the river from Che Guervera and his rebel guerilla army headquarters. We were so close to the enemy in both the cow pasture and in the new buildings that General Heath, Surgeon General of the Army, reportedly said of our situation in those positions it was "the first time to his knowledge that casualties had to be evacuated *to* the *front.*" Close enough that Captain Billy Wolfe and I had been chased naked down along the water's edge by mortar rounds when caught skinny-dipping in the ocean waves at the beach behind the fine estate formerly belonging to the family of General Trujillo, the Dominican Republic dictator, who no longer lived there. The hacienda wall had many spots where bullets had struck, the Dominicans said the bullet marks were from summary executions of many people who crossed Trujillo.

"When?" Every one asked. No one knew when Bob Hope would be arriving. Rumors varied from the next day to next month. No one seemed to have the real scoop, a typical scenario in the military. The buzz was that Hope was going to stage a televised USO show out at the captured Isidro Airport, and he would visit the wounded in the hospital while here. The *when* was not as important as the fact he *was* coming.

Eventually, Bob Hope did arrive with his entire troupe. The first show was as predicted, at Isidro Airfield, where a huge contingent of troops from the combined military services enjoyed the entertainment as it was being televised for one of his famous road shows for the armed services.

Hope did a comedy monologue to the delight of the thousands sitting or crouched on the tarmac ground. His famous line, "But, I want to tell you…." was in full swing. So was his golf club. Laughter is good for the soul and spirit; Hope evoked plenty of laughter. Tuesday Weld, the beautiful actress, performed a comedy dialogue routine with Hope. Joey Heatherton did an incredible gyrating sexy dance of acrobatic, jelly-shaking pelvic velocity while the troops "oohed" and "ahhed," and whistled, some pretending to swoon. The soldiers fell in love with her immediately, and fondly nick-named her "Joey the Crotch," indicating where some of their interest might lie.

Mustachioed Jerry Colonna did his famous high-pitched, bulging eyes routine. Famed guitarist Tony Romano played accompaniment. A lovely female singer sang wonderfully a peppy version of "Ten Fine Fingers." Sadly, I have forgotten her name. Frequent rippling peals of laughter erupted from the mesmerized servicemen throughout the entire show. Thunderous and extended applause from a grateful audience burst forth at the end of the show. I was fortunate to be among those applauding, whistling and cheering.

Hope's next stop was to be down in the guerilla-controlled area of Santo Domingo, where only a sandbag corridor was being kept open by our troops. It is impossible to heap too much praise on this unique man, Hope.

The 15th Hospital was pleased that Hope and his entourage came and walked among the wounded, giving a kind word or witty joke here and there. Hope spotted the name tag on the army green fatigue shirt of a good-looking blonde nurse whose last name was "Lays."

Hope said, "Your name is Lays, huh?" He turned aside toward the wounded in cots and wheelchairs, and joked, "I bet you guys wish she did, huh?" He got a bigger laugh than he expected. Some of the troops *wished* that she did, but most of the staff, especially the med evac pilots, and a number of the troops *knew* that she frequently *did*.

Bob Hope, Jerry Colonna, and Tony Romano sang a harmony rendition for the wounded and the medical staff. Bob was repeating some of his joke routine show when he suddenly forgot his next lines. A pregnant pause followed.

Tuesday Weld came to his rescue, stepped forward and said "You remember Bob, how you said…(and she gave him his lines)," Hope picked up on it and continued. Personally, I was aware of the miscue and the line, because I had heard the routines at the airfield show earlier. As a physician, I wondered if Bob Hope was truly getting into Stage One himself, with his own forgetfulness. He was not. (Later, decades of his spontaneous wit on talk shows like Johnny Carson's squashed that ridiculous theory.)

Bob Hope said, "I discovered there are three stages to getting old and becoming senile. Stage One is when you begin to forget names of things and of people you have met, especially recently. You know you have reached Stage Two when you forget to zip up the fly of your pants after use. (a pause here for a gesture the length of his trouser's fly, gets big laughs) But, I want to tell you…you know you have finally reached Stage Three when you forget to zip down *before* use." (the same gesture, in the opposite direction, gets even bigger laughs).

I dared to suggest, "There is a Stage Four, Mr. Hope. Stage Four is when you …when you…uh, when…uh…ah…I would tell you—if only I could remember it."

Hope grinned back at me, "Not bad, doc."

From time to time, an old black and white faded photograph takes me back to meeting Bob Hope, and like as not, into a journey reliving the paradoxical moments of tragedy and exhilaration, joy and sadness, the successes of saving many, and the pathos of crushing defeats I could not save. They were times shared with good men and women whose images emerge from my memory bank to live again like some staccato slide show.

The Santo Domingo, Dominican Republic, USO show of Bob Hope was filmed but, to my knowledge, never shown on public television. President Lyndon Johnson's ordered invasion of the D.R. was touchy, politically. Johnson later obtained the approval and participation of the Organization of American States (OAS), including Brazil, Honduras, Nicaragua and other Central and South American countries, which sent their soldiers to assist the troops of the United States. Criticism from Russia and her allies apparently provoked Johnson's administration to put the quietus on media publicity about Santo Domino. Maybe that contributed to the televised USO show never airing. Nevertheless, what counts is—BOB HOPE CAME.

SECOND OPINIONS

A rapping knock on the back door of my office door signaled another visitor at lunchtime. The opened door revealed the skinny, wasted frame of Bill Breward, a long-time attorney friend of medium stature with whom I had spent many happy times in the woods and fields with our dogs, sat by warming night fires on cold nights in lonely places, and swapped many a tall tale. His weight had gone down to only ninety-six pounds, and he had barely enough energy to struggle through each day of his law practice. The opinion in the community was Bill was dying of cancer or AIDS. They were wrong.

"Hey, Bill. Come on in and have a seat."

"Thanks. Got a few minutes?" Bill's usually smiling face appeared grim.

"For you? Sure. What's up?"

"I just got some more bad news, and I need a second opinion." He slumped down into the chair beside my desk, his brow wrinkled with worry.

Trying to lighten his mood, I responded, "Okay, here it is. You're ugly, and you drink too much beer. How's that for second opinions?"

He managed to materialize a grin, and said, "Nah, this time, I'm serious."

"Lay it out for me, Bill. What's going on?"

"I'm scheduled for three different major operations, starting next week, at West Paces Ferry Hospital, way on the other side of Atlanta."

"What?" The shock sobered any further attempts at humor. This was no joking matter.

Bill had come to me with a chronic recurring bladder infection. With the aid of a high index of suspicion, and studies with barium and dye studies, I had proven him to have a fistula (a leaking connection) between his lower colon and his bladder, the fecal contents of his colon leaking into his bladder causing the infections. Bill was sent to Dr. X, a Jewish urologist whom I respected, and to whom I referred many patients. Dr. X was to further confirm the extent of the leak, by using a cystoscope in his office to study from inside the bladder the size of the hole, and then return the patient to my further care.

"The first operation is supposed to be a colostomy, six weeks later remove my lower colon and a few months later close the colostomy." He named three doctors who were to do the surgery. Their names were unfamiliar to me, but I recognized by their names they were also likely Jewish.

"Who arranged all this?" My initial surprise was followed by anger at someone's interference in the care of my personal friend.

"The urologist."

"Stay right here, Bill. I'm going to call Dr. X." Using a telephone in the adjoining room, my call produced Dr. X, whom I asked rather curtly, "Bill Breward says you scheduled him for three operations with surgeons way on the other side of Atlanta. Why? By whom? Did you forget I am a surgeon, and that it was me that sent him to you? Bill is my patient and a close friend."

The reasoning behind his reply was disappointing, and saddened me. "Ernie, I knew these three young surgeons were just getting started over there and needed the business. I didn't think you would mind. I didn't stop to think about you being a surgeon. I'm sorry." (He neglected to add that the three young surgeons were of the same faith as his. All of my many practice years I observed this same behavior among people of his ilk. They welcomed referrals, but referred cases only to doctors of their same faith. I had thought better of Dr. X.)

"Your young doctors scheduled Bill for three surgeries. In the right hands, I believe it can be done in one operation, and save the patient time, money, and the risk of two extra operations: and that is what we are going to do. You can tell your young friends." The conversation dwindled down to polite farewells. I still respected the professional skills of Dr. X, and would continue to have my patients benefit from that skill, but I knew Dr.X would remain the same philosophically.

Because I want my patients to receive top care, my decisions were not based on religious or sect preferences, but on where I could improve their chances, if only by one per cent. That patient might prove to be the extra one out of a hundred to survive, and that would mean one hundred percent to him or her.

"Bill, you can forget about having all three operations, and about being so far away from your family. You are going to meet a colleague of mine, Doctor Bill Pendergrast, a terrific surgeon, and we are going to get you all fixed up with only one surgery needed." His face and attitude lightened up at that piece of news.

"When?" He was anxious now. "Let's get it over with."

"As soon as we have you properly prepared for surgery, not in any hasty rush. I really can't guarantee you that one surgery will do the job, Bill, because the connection is very low, near the end of the lower colon, at the rectum, and will be difficult to reach, but with the skilled hands of my colleague, Doctor Pendergrast being involved, your chances are real good for only one procedure being required."

"That sounds mighty good. Get on with it, let the dice roll." His cavalier response junction was a charade to mask his fatalistic attitude. This reinforced my suspicion that Bill secretly thought he actually had cancer and was dying, and I was only trying to comfort him. Along with all his friends, he expected us to find inoperable cancer and that he was doomed.

The surgery was successfully performed in only one stage, despite the precarious position of the fistulous opening, so very low, at the rectum-colon junction. It was touch and go, but Doctor Pendergrast, with his magical hands, made all the difference, reaching, excising and repairing such a low-lying anastomosis (re-joining the colon). It was not a job for the average surgeon.

Bill survived, gained weight, went back to his law practice, and his good humor.

The knock on my office back door signaled Bill had arrived for one of our frequent lunchtime crossword puzzle challenge races. While munching parched peanuts which Bill often brought, we took two copies of the daily newspaper puzzle and started the race to see who could finish their copy first, winner take all the peanuts.

"You know," he said, placing his puzzle aside, "My wife said you must be a pretty good surgeon. You want a second opinion?"

"Sure."

"You're ugly, too." We both laughed, and it was good to be alive.

The Folly Of Required Second Opinions (RSO's)

First, I believe at least ninety-five percent of first opinions are honestly given by dependable honest physicians trying their best to be of valued service, are correct, and are without the need for second opinions. Of the remaining five per cent maybe four and one-half per cent are also honestly given, but conceivably could be questioned as to whether the procedure is the only, or best, approach. The remaining one-half per cent (or less) are the "rotten apples" in our medical barrel, which we are constantly trying to weed out. Because they exist, second opinions can sometimes be valuable

It is well and good for a person who wishes to obtain a second opinion to do so, and seek the relief it implies. Use common sense, and be wise. Do not accept for a second opinion a doctor recommended by the first physician. Be sure your choice has a good reputation and has no relationship of any kind with the first doctor. It would also help if your second physician is fearless and has enough strength of character to stand his ground later, if required. I know from experience, for I spoke the truth when asked.

In the high majority of cases, I believe, it has become obvious that requiring second opinions (RSO) of patients is fruitless. Such second opinions are usually worthless, a waste of time and money, and contribute little, if any, to the assurance that the first opinion is indeed justified and correct. They also increase the cost of medical care and insurance premiums, and are far from being protective of patients.

Too often, the second opinion is rendered by an associate who belongs to the same medical group, or by a physician acquainted with the first physician through friendship or by being affiliated on the same hospital staffs. Even an independent physician in the same community will think twice before he contradicts the first doctor's recommendation, for fear of excommunication of himself by the medical community, as well as the very real possibility of being sued by the first physician for defamation of his professional character and reputation.

Whether by state law, hospital or insurance company mandates, a required second opinion (RSO) is like legislation that demands a "butterfly" band-aid be placed on all lacerations—what if the laceration is a severed major artery, such as the aorta? Idiotic.

Required second opinions (RSO) are also self-serving for the insurance company, as well as the politicos who legislate their requirement.

How? First, can anyone seriously believe the insurance company only raises their premium costs to exactly offset the extra cost of the second opinion, and does not add for the company an additional profit? Secondly, the state politicos can gain personal benefit by being able to proclaim, "See what we have done for you. We created this legislation to protect you." The hospital that requires second opinions can benefit, in the face of some malpractice action, distancing themselves by posturing, "See, it's not our fault, we require second opinions."

And the band plays on, the music of their manipulations swelling into a crescendo.

DESTINY AND DYNAMITE

The lights of our three-car caravan cruising down the lonely two-lane highway formed an ellipse of the roadbed that looked like a never-ending teepee in front of the car, the center line representing the doorway flap. Three cars were full of determined grown men and one 14 year-old boy, heading south from Atlanta and bound for Jonesboro, Georgia, with a single purpose.

The men were from Georgia Power Company, and played in the "fast-pitch" Industrial League. Their softball team was en route to play a night game. About ninety minutes were required in those days to traverse the approximately twenty-five miles. I was that fourteen year-old youth, and I was the third baseman.

Many years later Jonesboro would become part of Metropolitan Atlanta. I would have an experience this night that would develop into a hilarious outcome more than twenty-five years later.

My mind was occupied with more immediate concerns, however. I was hungry. I was thinking, "Man, that black walnut Spinning Wheel that Charlie bought me was about the best thing I ever tasted." A Spinning Wheel was an ice cream concoction, spun similar to a milk shake.

It was just about dark when the cars pulled into the Miss Georgia in the Atlanta parking lot and stopped. "Charlie, I asked, "how did they get the name Miss Georgia?" He didn't know, and none of the other men did either. I never did find out how the dairy and ice cream shop got the name, but never forgot that sweet introduction to their product, as this tale gives testimony.

"E. W.," Charlie asked, "you want a Spinning Wheel?" They called me that in those childhood days. Too proud to admit I did not know what he was talking about, I said, warily, "I guess so." The men entered the shop and I tagged along, curious.

"What flavor do you want in yours?" Charlie asked me. I could see they were all ordering from a list of flavors on the wall.

"Black Walnut," I answered, like I had been ordering Spinning Wheels all of my life.

The girl behind the counter poured milk into a container, dipped ice cream and added it, then squirted some juice on top, put it in a spinning apparatus and served it up. The first taste immediately told me I had chosen well. "This is great, Charlie. Thanks."

"Think nothing of it, kid," he replied, "my treat."

We got to the ball field, and there was one shock after another. There were no fences. On a rise behind the outfielders, there was a two-story brick, run-down, small building that looked like it had existed unchanged since Lee surrendered at Appomattox back on April 9, 1865. The opposing players said it was the local high school. The night was as black as a sheet of black velvet in a midnight unlit room, and the field had only three lights. One light was on a pole behind home plate, one light was on a pole beside third base, where I played, and one light was on a pole beside first base.

In warming up, I discovered right away that any ball hit into the sky would disappear into the great abyss of the black darkness above the lights and be lost from sight. Where it would fall was anybody's guess, which made for a Keystone Cop kind of slapstick ball game. The poor outfielders were worse off than anybody. They never had a chance. When a fly ball was hit up into the dark, you would see them either run around like a chicken with its head cut off, or take a step or two, then stand still. The ball would come down out of the dark and hit, "plop," somewhere out there on the ground. They would then run to fetch the ball and relay it in to the infielders.

As if that wasn't bad enough, there was more, and this was the real clincher. Our guy, Dave, was the first batter and hit a grounder into the hole between short and third. The shortstop got to it and made a nice throw. Dave was legging it down to first base with all the speed he could muster. It was a close play, but Dave was called out. His speed was still up as he turned right into the foul territory along the right field line.

Suddenly, Dave started acrobatics, arms flailing and legs jumping like he was being attacked by a swarm of wasps, or maybe a big snake. That's when we saw the big splashes of water flying up into the air, just as Dave went down hard.

We ran out there johnny-quick to see what happened and if he was okay. When we got there, Dave was sitting in a swamp of water, looking like a soaked Baptist fresh out of the baptismal tank after being dunked, and he was mad as a wet banty hen.

To our surprise, the area between the right field line and the parallel road that ran about sixty to eighty feet away was a water-filled swamp. The size was not enough to compare to the Okefenokee Swamp, nor was the degree of disorder. There were no gators or cypress trees, but I bet you a dollar to a doughnut there were snakes somewhere in that water. And there was Dave still sitting down in it, hot as a firecracker, and his teammates laughing at the sight.

By now, you may be wondering what the heck a fourteen year-old child's baseball game has to do with medicine and a doctor's memoirs. Well, as I would have said back then, "hold your taters," here it comes.

Judge Ed Kemp stood up at the Exchange Club meeting being held in the Lake Spivey Country Club, in the same Jonesboro, where I was now practicing medicine. He said, "They say confession is good for the soul. I want to share a story with you from nearly twenty-five years ago, a story I have never before told anyone."

Judge Kemp was a tall man, thin, with sharp facial features, and a long sharp nose to go with it. He was a well-respected member of the community, a co-founder of the newspaper, and a civic leader, born and raised in Jonesboro where he now served Clayton County as a Superior Court Judge. He was a good storyteller, so we expected something special.

"Many years ago," he started, "beside what is now the Little League baseball field, there was a swamp running in the foul territory alongside the first base line all the way out beside the outfield. It had been there a long time, and was a real eyesore. Every effort to drain it had failed up till the time that I decided to take the task in hand myself."

He stopped, as any good storyteller would, once he had the interest of his audience, and took a sip from a nearby glass of water.

"Well, I got a friend of mine and we judged, no pun intended, the best thing to do would be to dynamite the swamp, and just blow it up to kingdom come. Surely, if anything was still left of the swamp, it would then drain easily."

This story was getting more interesting, especially for me, for I remembered the swamp from my visit there to play in the softball game twenty-five years earlier.

"So we took the dynamite down there one Saturday about the middle of the day, set it up where we guessed it would do the most good, got to a safe distance, and prepared to be lauded as the heroes of the town for solving the unsightly swamp problem."

He took another sip of water, now that he definitely had his audience hooked and anxious to know the outcome of exploding the dynamite.

Judge Kemp continued, "Right across the street on the east side of the ball field, just across from the right field fence was a house. I don't remember to whom the house belonged. It was one of those houses called a "shotgun" house, you know, where it is longer from front to back than from side to side, with a middle hallway running down the length of the house, starting from the front door and going all the way to the back door.

For you younger folks, it was called a "shotgun" house because back in the moonshine days, a shotgun fired through the open front door would carry the whole length of the house and do considerable, deadly damage." I recalled that in New Orleans, during my surgery residency there, I had heard the same term used, for the same descriptive reason.

"We didn't have any idea how much dynamite to use. We concluded it was better to have a little too much, rather than to use too little, which led us to an unpredictable, unforgettable conclusion." He paused, and gauged his effect, so far, upon the listeners.

"You never saw such a sight in your life as when that dynamite went off," he continued. "Mud, swamp water, weeds, rocks, trees and spindly branch sticks burst out of an enormous exploding fireball, and cascaded down not only all over the field, but the road and surrounding territory, including the "shotgun" house across the street. Within a few seconds, it seemed like a hundred or more black people were running from that house in every direction, and they kept running, nonstop." A titter of surprised laughter broke out among his audience. "Some ran past where Lee street school is now, some up past the Jonesboro Bank, others toward Tara Boulevard; in other words, in every direction. It looked like the Charge of the Black Brigade, to paraphrase Mr. Kipling."

His conclusion produced the desired effect; smiles, appreciative comments, and a smattering of light laughter.

Judge Kemp was still standing when I arose. "Pardon me, Judge Kemp, with your permission, I may be able to add some further enlightenment to your story."

He looked puzzled. I knew what he was thinking. How could this newcomer, here only five or six years, know anything about that swamp and the dynamite?

Finally, he said, "Let's hear it."

While standing beside my place at the long table, I began, "To begin with, I am familiar with that swamp, up close and personal. I visited Jonesboro, more than twenty-five years ago, as a lad of fourteen to play third base for a men's team from Atlanta." I bet that surprised everybody, I thought.

"Well, Judge, that house you are talking about is the one where Eddie Lemons and his family used to live, where the new library now stands, right?"

"Yes, I know," the Judge replied. He looked puzzled.

"Eddie, Willie and all the Lemons are patients of mine. Eddie and I were talking together about the old days in Jonesboro when the subject of my 1947 visit for a softball game arose. I mentioned the experience of Dave and the swamp along first base. That's when Eddie told me about an incident with an explosion that happened years ago."

The Judge's look of puzzlement now transformed to one of intense interest.

"He described to me what happened," I continued, "as he personally experienced it when your dynamite exploded, Judge. I'm not sure you know his side of the story. Eddie told me about the explosion many years ago near his house, but he only seemed to know there had been an explosion, and no further details except how it affected his home."

It was easy to tell the Judge was unsure as to what I was about to reveal. His intensity was now mixed with raised eyebrows, accompanying a rise in expectant curiosity.

"Judge, what you didn't know at the time, was that they were having a wedding in that "shotgun" house. There were a hundred or more people attending the wedding and festivities. Eddie said to me, "When that big explosion occurred outside our house, we thought the Ku Klux Klan had done tried to blow us up, or the end of the world had come. The whole side of our long house, the side on the opposite side from the ball field, fell out into the yard. We all run for our lives."

Now, there was another burst of laughter among the Exchange Club attendees,

The look of surprise on the Judge's face was reward enough for me. A slow grin eased into the makeup of his face, and he said, "I never heard about that until this day. We caught a lot of grief in the community for our precipitous, but ill-fated, attempt. It didn't cure the swamp either, but years later it was finally eliminated."

"I suspected maybe you hadn't heard Eddie's side of the story," I said.

"No, I never did. We were young and ambitious fools, but well-intentioned. It was a different time, too. These days, we would be arrested and in serious trouble for doing such a dumb thing."

All is well that ends well, I suppose. The young man with the good intentions, but faulty judgment, grew up to be a respected judge. With the money the county paid the Lemons family for their land, they built several homes down the paved street on the other side of the ball field, which is now a modern, high-end Little League Complex and Park. The county built a modern library on the land purchased from the Lemons family.

Ultimately, the story evolved into a "win-win" situation for everyone.

ROSE AND THE MARUYAMA VACCINE

One of the silent, insidious, and most dangerous of illnesses that women must face is cancer of the ovaries, usually too far advanced by metastatic spread before the first symptoms appear.

My friend, Rose, a vivacious, personable lady and accomplished artist was in her middle fifties. She came to see me, and said, "Doctor, my stomach has been causing severe pain, and is swollen. It's been going on for a month or more." A worried look broke through the usually smiling and pleasant countenance I was accustomed to seeing upon the face of Rose. She was not the sort of patient who complained about petty or imagined symptoms. For some unexplained reason, I felt a sense of foreboding.

Six or seven years previously, as she neared fifty years of age, Rose had a hysterectomy performed by some unknown military surgeon who had left her ovaries intact. If a woman has had her children already, or is past the child-bearing age, it is advisable to remove the ovaries at the time of a hysterectomy for fear ovarian cancer might develop later.

Sadly, my investigation and ultimate surgery for Rose determined that she had advanced cancer of the ovaries with innumerable, widespread metastatic implants throughout her abdominal cavity and organs, making a surgical remedy inoperable, and impossible. The spread was so severe that her life expectancy was estimated to be only in terms of a few weeks, with an outside chance for possibly a couple of months.

At that time, there was essentially nothing available except pain medications for an advanced state of widespread cancer as in Rose's case. Few would have even tried anything heroic beyond that point, preferring to give the patient total pain relief and comfort, as well as time to get their final affairs in order, and for their families to be together.

But Rose was filled with courage, matter-of-factness, and a determined lady. She had been a sergeant in the German Luftwaffe in World War II, married a U.S. Army sergeant, became an American citizen, raised a family, and became the darling of our community, loved by all. Rose wanted to try every possible available means to delay or cure the illness, and encouraged me to search the medical literature and make inquiries for all possibilities.

Professor Maruyama at the University of Tokyo had developed an experimental vaccine showing promise of being effective in cancer of the ovary, and possibly, to a lesser extent, in other cancers such as malignant melanoma. He had observed that cancer rarely, if ever, occurred in lepers in a Pacific leprosy colony, and also apparently not in tuberculosis patients. Applying that reasoning, he developed a vaccine from those two sources, lepers and tuberculosis patients. The results of his early research seemed very promising. Rose and I were in desperate straits at this stage, so I contacted Professor Maruyama, explained the case and asked for his assistance.

In order to get the vaccine into the United States for medical use, permission had to be obtained from the U.S. Food and Drug Administration. After talking with Rose and explaining everything available that I could, this brave lady encouraged me to apply for the Maruyama program with the FDA. I immediately applied.

The Food and Drug Administration approved my application, as well as approving and appointing five (5) other physicians in different parts of the United States to begin a similar undertaking. We were to conduct a trial research program of the Maruyama Vaccine, but were required to limit our patients to be used only for those patients already in *extremis gravis* condition, expected to die is a few short weeks or months. This certainly would not be a fair trial therefore, but Rose and I were like "clutching at straws in a drowning whirlpool of water." We accepted the limitations, glad for any kind of a chance to save her.

Professor Maruyama worked closely with us, and incredibly, in Rose's case, she improved steadily over the next few months, which then stretched into more than a year. Nearly a year and a half later, just as we were beginning to feel very good about her prognosis, Rose began to have distention of her abdomen, which proved to be fluid that required puncturing her abdomen and inserting tubes to drain off the ascites fluid. This was ominous, and I now suspected the worst. It indicated the cancer was now overcoming the vaccine, and beginning to defeat us. More and more frequently, she swelled and we would drain off more fluid, the interval between episodes becoming progressively shorter, and the quantities of fluid increasing greatly. We cried together many times.

We both recognized that this course we were forced to follow was indicating an inevitable conclusion, but we continued the fight. Rose grew weaker with each episode. Finally, this woman of indomitable spirit, spoke to me as I came once again to her hospital bedside, ready to again drain fluid. The pain had increased steadily in severity the last few months. Her abdomen was swollen to the point that she was in severe agony, despite all of our efforts to block pain.

She looked me straight in the eyes and pleaded, "Let me go, Ernest, let me go, please let me go." We both broke down and cried, two friends recognizing the truth. "I beg you, just let me go." Rose had reached the end of her courageous fight. She knew it, and I knew it, too. I leaned over her hospital bed, cheek to cheek, and we held each other as tightly as we could in her weakened condition. We sobbed and cried together. (as I must again, while writing these words).

All I could do was continue to ease her pain and discomfort as much as possible those final moments, and Rose departed this life. Once again, a little of me died, too. Her spirit abides with me still. She gave me her painting of a pair of worn-out, old work boots, a constant reminder of the courage of my friend, Rose.

Her courage, however, led to something worthwhile for others. The FDA received all of the case reports for my part of the research. I made notations that the vaccine stretched the "terminal" few weeks for Rose into nearly two years, and suggested they approve further studies, but to include starting patients with *early* detected cancers. I was never informed as to whether they did that or not, and have seen no reports to that effect.

From the research came good news, however. Professor Maruyama's vaccine had apparently keyed other significant research. Several university medical schools in the United States, including the University of Georgia, were proclaiming later they had made significant advances in research for treatment of malignant melanoma by the administration and use of an aberrant form of the tubercular portion of Maruyama's vaccine. If Rose knew that her courage had been a factor in the advance of knowledge that would later benefit many others, I think she would probably say, "Thank God."

❋ ❋ ❋

Death has long grasping tentacles that reach out to drain life from the human body in various and sundry ways. Regardless of the different circumstances, the result is always the same. Finally, we must all slip into that mysterious journey from life into non-life. The doctor's commitment is to try to prevent that from happening. He should be dedicated to the proposition that it is possible to thrust death from the doorway.

The Grim Reaper, has been my nemesis throughout my professional life, my eternal combatant foe, against which I have pitched many vigorous battles. When you have been a part of pulling someone back from the brink of death's reaching hand, of having been victorious in one these struggles, there comes a glorious feeling of satisfaction, and a giving of thanks unto God for the gift of your knowledge or skill, as well as for the good fortune of the patient.

Of course, some battles cannot be won, nor delayed. That is the other side of the coin, so to speak. How tortuous and depressive the feelings are when you cannot win the battle to save a patient, or give them a reprieve. You suffer down deep in your soul, with constant self-introspection, worrying if anything could have been done differently to obtain a different result. The cumulative toll of these cases upon a caring physician can break his spirit, like a soldier in the front lines too long, and he may become a "burnt-out case."

MOLLY'S MALADY

"Look at the pictures of my children, Doctor. Aren't they beautiful?" Molly extended the photographs to me with the natural proud look of a happy parent, her eyes shining lustrously as they beamed at me. Molly was a jolly, hugely obese, thirty year-old lady with brown hair, blue eyes, and a pleasantness in her manner that warmed everyone she met to her, including our entire office staff.

"You certainly have a fine looking boy and girl. I'm sorry, but their names have slipped my mind." Molly always brought photographs to show the growth of her children, and some of their interesting activities. The kids had a pediatrician for their medical care, so I had never seen them in person.

"Without a moment's hesitation, she replied "Mark and Teresa. Teresa made the honor roll at school." She added, "I'm lucky to have such a wonderful husband, too. He is so good to me."

"Yes, you have mentioned that before. He truly must be a patient and caring man." In fact, Molly always kept the office staff informed about how her kids were doing at school or in extracurricular activities, and how her husband was so kind and attentive to her. Her sweet personality endeared her to all of our office staff. We enjoyed seeing the pictures each visit and hearing Mark's successes in Little League and how Teresa was doing. Molly was a friendly, likeable person, making it easy for us to over-sympathize with Molly about her obesity.

"Oh, he is. James does the grocery shopping, the housework and the cooking. I don't know what I would do without him, being overweight like I am."

Overweight? Massive is the word. Molly's exact weight was unknown. Our scales only registered up to 350 pounds. When Molly stepped on our scales, the measurement immediately jumped past the 350 mark and headed toward infinity. She weighed somewhere between 450 and 550 pounds we speculated, carried on a 4 foot 10 inch frame. Her thighs and upper arms looked like giant ham hocks. As she waddled down the hallway in our office her enormous buttocks would almost touch both walls on the sides of the passageway at the same time. Her thin cotton "mumu" dresses draped over her like a giant open parachute had been dropped from above to land and cover her completely all the way to the floor, the edges dragging the floor as she walked. Store-bought clothing to accommodate her size was not likely to be found. Various endocrinology consultants had been of no help.

"If I could lose weight, I wouldn't have this pain I came today to tell you about."

"What pain? The knees and hips?" I presumed she was referring to joint pain in the knee, hip or back from carrying so much weight around.

"In my stomach." My presumption changed from joints to gastrointestinal causes.

"I guess I'll have to show you." With that she tried to bend forward and reach the hem of her garment, but could not. Alternatively, Molly began to reel in her dress front by pulling a few feet of the garment at a time until a shocking surprise unfolded before my eyes. This unfortunate lady had an abdomen so ponderous that it was overlapping her pubic area and hanging down like a separate appendage until it reached the floor where she stood. "I've had it for weeks, but now it's getting worse. The pain is at the bottom where my stomach touches the floor, where I can't see it," she said.

Neither could I. Nurse Brenda and I were able to struggle Molly into a position leaning back against the examining table and using leverage to bring the undersurface into view. Inspection revealed the cause of her pain. It was not a pretty sight. Her abdomen, by dragging the floor as she walked, had eroded an area, about 19 centimeters by 9 centimeters. Contact with the floor had caused the loss of skin and the underlying soft tissues down to the fascia of the muscles, where a purulent exudate of infection was present throughout the shallow, linear trench.

"Molly, dear," I said, "Your pain is because you have infection and have destroyed some of the tissue at the bottom of your abdomen, the part that hangs over. This has been caused by dragging your stomach against the floor and carpet when you are walking. Even when you are just sitting, I notice, it still rests against the floor, causing more pressure."

She looked up in despair, her usual countenance of pleasantness vanished, her brow wrinkled.

She asked, anxiously, "Can it be fixed? What am I going to do? I have to walk, to look after my sweet family."

"Your infection can be controlled, but not if the irritation by contact and dragging continues. The lost tissue is going to take many weeks to heal. That is, if we can keep you off your feet for that length of time." That did not seem likely. I tried to think of other ways.

"What am I going to do? James and the children need me. I can't stay in the bed for weeks." Her eyes became watery, and her hands began to writhe and twist together as if she was washing them.

"I don't know, maybe a soft tissue skin graft would do, after the infection is controlled. No, on second thought, returning to dragging the floor would destroy the grafted tissue again, and you would be right back where you are now." Her watery eyes began to stream tears down her face.

It was at that moment an idea popped into the equation. "I have an idea, let me make a call. I'll be back in a few minutes."

Dr. Bill Pendergrast, one of the very best of the skilled abdominal surgeons with whom I had ever operated, came to his telephone in response to my call. Molly's problem was discussed in detail, as was my "brainstorm." We agreed the probability of a recurrence was likely if treated only by local measures to heal the infection and by grafting, because the abdomen would still be dragging the floor. We felt we stood a much better chance if we could perhaps remove the *cause,* the protuberant hanging abdominal appendage, which was the etiology in the first place.

The idea was explained to Molly, including the risk that the abdomen might later repeat the development of a similar overlapping, hanging abdomen, as well as the risks of surgery in general. Local treatment with antibiotics and grafting was the other option, and explained fully. The choice was left up to Molly.

"I'll have to talk it over with my husband, James, first." she said.

"And you should," of course," I replied. "Just let me know what you decide."

Molly and her husband chose the surgery to remove the huge hanging abdominal excess of adipose, fatty tissue. She was admitted to the hospital, all the necessary forms were completed, and the surgery was performed without incident. She went home, still obese, but with an abdomen no longer dragging the floor.

Bill and I met again in the hospital a few weeks later, and we were talking about the Molly's case when he asked, "Did you hear how much the part we removed weighed?"

"No, I didn't. How much?"

"One hundred and fifty-eight pounds."

"Whew, but I'm not too surprised. It seemed like more to me. By the way, I never saw visitors in her room, not even her husband, did you?"

"Her husband? She doesn't have a husband." You could have knocked me over with a napkin.

"What? Who are you kidding? She has been my patient for years. My office staff and I have seen many pictures of her husband, James, and her children as they grew older."

"She doesn't have any children either. She's never been married."

This was almost too much to swallow. "How do you know that?"

"Her registration form lists no husband to contact in the event of an emergency. Since you had mentioned her husband and kids before surgery, I confronted her. She confessed it was true. She confided to me that she expected no one would ever marry her because of her weight, and the next best thing was for her to have a fantasy family."

I had to accept that I had been gulled, led down a primrose path, sucker punched, conned, fooled completely like B'rer Rabbit by the Tar-Baby of B'rer Fox. On further consideration, however, I could sympathize. Her husband and her children, sadly, were a figment of her imagination, an attempt to compensate for the probability that she was unlikely to ever enjoy that kind of relationship. Molly's mental mechanism for compensating for that loss may be a good thing for her, as it is likely she is correct and going to remain single, unmarried.

At any rate, the last time I saw Molly for follow-up of her surgery, she still tipped the scales well over the three hundred and fifty pound limit of our scales. Adding the one hundred and fifty-eight pounds removed to the weighing today means Molly weighed over five hundred pounds pre-operatively. She brought no pictures to the office this visit, made no references to her "family," but was as cheerful as usual. I suspect she was embarrassed by the subterfuge she had practiced upon us—after this office visit, I never saw Molly again.

THE INCOMPETENT

During Internal Medicine training at Johns Hopkins, a rotation was required out to Baltimore City Hospital, a dismal gray edifice resembling a massive mausoleum more than a hospital. The patient clientele differed from Hopkins in that no celebrities or affluent people frequented Baltimore City Hospital, (BCH). It was a general hospital, but with one large section of the hospital strictly for geriatric patients, a large percentage of which had suffered cerebrovasular accidents, (strokes) that seemed more suitable for nursing home care than long term residents of a hospital. However, this was in a time before "Long-term Care" (read that as "expensive" and "bankrupting") became the standard.

The rotation for six weeks to BCH, I believe, was to broaden our experience by encountering a different strata of patients and illnesses. As far as teaching us, it did not accomplish much. After the first few dozens patients with "strokes," the repetition becomes redundant. Nevertheless, I certainly learned something of value about myself, and about the unreliability of "credentials."

The Intensive Care Unit was crowded as usual with patients in all kinds of serious predicaments. The idea of separate Medical and Surgical ICU's had not yet come about, so the mix was complicated. It was the middle of the night as I walked into the ICU to check on William Walker, a myocardial infarct (heart attack) patient of mine admitted earlier. I was immediately aware there was an air of tension in the room. The eyes of the nurses were darting alternately among themselves and frantically back and forth towards a bed near the center of the large area.

Before I could speak, one of the nurses hurried to my side, glanced in the direction of the same bed, and whispered, "Please, doctor, see if you can help the other doctor, we are in danger of losing the patient. They're losing lots of blood."

I guessed she was reacting to my white coat, not knowing I was only a lowly first year Internal Medicine level, not Surgery. "What's going on?"

"He's trying to do a tracheotomy. He's been at it over an hour, the bleeding is getting bad, and he's can't control it."

"Who is he?"

"He's the Chief Resident in Surgery. Please help. Hurry.'"

The Chief Resident in Surgery was having trouble with a tracheotomy? Unbelievable. I looked quickly at the scenario. Curtains had been drawn aside, exposing a man and two nurses leaning over, surrounding the bedside. I noticed the sheets were splattered with blood, streaks beginning to work down their sides in tiny rivulets. The man was wearing a white lab coat and a surgical mask. I walked over and peered over his shoulder at the site of surgery. It could not be seen for the copious amount of blood welling out of the incision opening. His sleeves were bloody. I noticed the doctor was trying to perform the tracheotomy from the patient's left-hand side and the doctor was handling instruments right-handedly, an awkward situation. He glanced at me for a second with no recognition, fear clearly visible in his eyes, returned to shakily sticking hemostat clamps down into the gushing pool of blood, where he could not possibly see what he was grabbing. It did not take a genius to recognize he was in a panic and did not know what he was doing. The two nurses looked at me, searching my eyes, pleading.

"Need a hand?" I asked. No reply came to my offer. "I worked in surgery at Emory several years." He was too panic-stricken to reply, busily diving into the welling blood with clamps.

Somebody, I thought, had better do something, and right now. He's out of control. Without asking anybody for any further permission, I donned a mask, gown, and gloves, stepped up to the bed on the patient's right-hand side, opposite the doctor, and just took over. The Chief Resident did not resist me, obviously glad to be relieved and let somebody else take the responsibility. Packing the wound tightly with laparotomy pads of thick gauze and holding pressure for several minutes significantly diminished the bleeding enough to permit close inspection by sneaking past one tiny edge of the packing at a time. *My God, it looks like the guy has the left lobe of the thyroid gland macerated and bleeding from his grabbing at bleeders. No, geez, it looks like he has mistakenly tried to go right through the lobe itself in his search for the trachea. Doesn't he know anatomy any better than that?*

His incision had been misplaced, and he was wide of the mark laterally. Standing in his awkward position, on the wrong side of the table, had misled him straight into "Dangersville." The thyroid is an extremely vascular gland. Unknowingly, the doctor had wandered directly into it. I controlled the bleeders systematically until the field was no longer a crisis. Except for some loss of thyroid tissue, the lobe was otherwise effectively spared. The incision was extended in order to more accurately approach the trachea. The trachea was identified and opened with a scalpel, a giant gush of air preceding the insertion of the tracheotomy tube, which was then connected to a respirator and oxygen.

The ordeal was over. We walked away from the bed and into the hallway. In order to support a sagging ego, the Chief Resident in Surgery assumed an arrogant countenance upon his face, took an aggressive pose resting one fist upon his hip, and said defiantly, "I didn't need you to stick your nose in it, you know. It was just a simple trach." Complete denial is a handy mental mechanism of defense when one needs it.

"Well, I wasn't sure, and I had nothing else to do anyway." I let him off the hook gently as I could.

Puzzled as to why a Chief Resident in Surgery mangled so badly such a relatively common procedure, I decided the next day to inquire around about him. Baltimore City Hospital was a full teaching hospital of the University of Maryland Medical School (and also of Hopkins for ancillary Internal Medicine). I was stunned by what I learned. Before coming to BCH, he had served a surgery residency at The Peter Bent Brigham Hospital, a very highly regarded Boston hospital affiliated with Harvard University. His M.D. degree had been obtained from the medical school at the State University of New York. His credentials were impeccable. His skill was not.

The real clincher about this guy came a few days later, just before my rotation back to Hopkins. I walked into the Procto Clinic area where a proctoscopic exam was about to be performed. A group of medical students from the University of Maryland School of Medicine were gathered about the same Chief Resident in Surgery of tracheotomy fame. He was instructing them in the use of the proctoscope.

I decided to stay for the show. I heard him say, "There is nothing difficult about placing the proctoscope perfectly to examine the sigmoid colon. It is so easy you don't even have to look in the scope as it passes. There are three simple turns to make. Without looking, you can pass from the rectum to the rectosigmoid junction, and then into the sigmoid colon. These three simple movements will by-pass the rugal folds at each of the turning points."

At this point, he grasped a proctoscope and showed his three prescribed movements, waving the scope in the air to demonstrate the required angles. The students seemed suitably impressed. I was not.

"Follow me now" he continued, "and I shall demonstrate what I have just told you. I have a clinic patient whose procto appointment is today and has agreed to participate in your teaching." He led the medical students through a doorway into an examining area for the instructive exhibition. Having never been enlightened in my medical training with regard to his three "blind" movements, and having observed the tracheotomy fiasco, I decided I wouldn't miss this for a ticket to see a Baltimore Colts game with Johnny Unitas, Raymond Berry, and Gino Marchetti. I tagged along with the rest of the crowd.

We entered the room where the patient was already prepared, upon the table in a facedown, prone "jackknife" position, with the feet lowered and the buttocks elevated, covered by draped sheets. The doctor spotted me in the crowd of students, paused for effect, as if to say, "Watch *this*, Buster." He turned triumphantly to the students, and said, "Watch closely."

He stepped to the table, opened the drapes slightly, just enough to expose the rear of the patient for the instrument required, picked up the proctoscope and turned to the students again. "Remember the three turns I described? I will now perform the same procedure." He looked directly at me once again, one eyebrow raised, the look upon his face best described as one of supreme satisfaction and superiority.

Placing the tip of the lubricated proctoscope at the opening, and without so much as a change in his erect standing posture, he slowly inserted the end an inch, then stopped to regale his audience once again. "Now, with the three simple motions, I begin…one…uh…two…uh"(he seemed to be having difficulty). "Three !" (at last, victorious)

He scanned his audience proudly, then singled me out. "Doctor," he said sarcastically, "would you be kind enough to inspect this for the students?" He did not want to miss this chance to gain full redemption in my eyes for his blunder in the tracheotomy. This would obviously put me in my place.

Reluctantly, put on the spot in front of the medical students, I nodded and walked to the table, prepared to do the deed. The scope must have been one of the extra long ones, I noticed, a goodly amount was still protruding outside the body. I did not have to look into the scope because a closer external look was quite sufficient to explain why the Chief Resident in Surgery had difficulty completing his "easy, three-step, blind proctoscopic approach to sigmoidoscopy of the colon."

There was no way out for me, I had to tell him right there in front of the students, "I'm sorry to tell you, doctor, but you have proctoscoped a vagina."

Indirectly, the tracheotomy incident had helped crystallize my decision about proceeding into the field of surgery upon completing the Internal Medicine at Johns Hopkins. It seemed to me I had a natural affinity and the skills required for surgery along with a helpful "calm in the face of calamity" demeanor. It remained to be seen if my assumptions would prove to be correct. I believed that surgery would prove to be the best way for me to be of service as a doctor. Making that kind of decision is also a doctor's responsibility to the public, and to himself. Do what you can do best, and do your best at it.

There is no doubt in my mind that this Chief Resident with his impeccable Harvard-related credentials ultimately practiced surgery in some unsuspecting locale. Undoubtedly, there is a certificate upon his wall showing that he was "certified" and approved by the American Board of Surgery, based on his fine background and the passing of a *written/oral examination*. Sadly, no one from the Board ever inspected or examined him in the operating room to see if he could actually perform *real* surgery. Pity the poor people. Shame to the system.

It was at BCH that I had my first inkling as to the heresy of "certifying" surgeons with only a written and oral exam, yet never seeing if the applicant could actually perform *real* surgery competently. The Chief Resident in Surgery was the beginning of that suspicion.

This fault in the system still exists more than fifty years later. On the office wall of your surgeon you may see his American Board of Surgery Certificate, but no member of the Board actually checked the applicant out as to his surgical ability before issuing the certificate. About the time I came to Hopkins, any kind of Board Certification was a relatively new thing, mostly beginning to gather steam after World War II, and was not yet important. The beginning of "certification" had started only a few years before the war, the idea being to replace the traditional apprenticeship system.

First, the "old boys" of long-standing in surgery had decided to require four years of surgery residency in a program of their approval, although the ones deciding this did not have to do that previously themselves. They decided to call their new organization the American Board of Surgery. Completion of four years surgery residency in an approved university teaching program made the young doctor Board Qualified and nothing further was required. The new surgeon was welcome at all hospitals. Sounds good, doesn't it, but politics inevitably entered the picture. Small private, non-teaching, non-university hospitals in the hinterlands entered the picture, desiring the "bragging rights" of having a surgical residency, if only for one position. These hospitals could also utilize the "surgery resident" in many ways, at the same time rejoicing in the traditional meager outlay of remuneration for his labors. This type of resident, after experiencing four years only assisting private practice surgeons, and with little or no formal teaching, was now "Board Qualified," but obviously was inadequate to actually perform surgery himself.

Next, a few of the same "old boys" had come up with the idea among themselves almost as sort of a new club, by which they would have the power to approve the "newcomers." Ultimately, I was to become Board Qualified in General Surgery, but when the date for my written/oral exam came to receive Board *Certification* it was scheduled in Puerto Rico and I was busily engaged in combat surgery overseas with the U.S. Army at the time. I had my duty to do and I was not dismayed. Board Qualified was all that was needed anywhere. Time would slowly change that

In the early days of the American Board of Surgery's existence, you could think of it as being approved to get your union card, only in this case your approvers were your competition. That compares to letting the fox already in the hen house decide who will be allowed to eat chickens, or to Oldsmobile deciding whether Henry Ford could start making automobiles. A union steward might use the term "closed shop."

Admittedly, close supervision and a viable means of certifying the budding surgeon is necessary, and the modern version of the American Board of Surgery has performed that task admirably, with one exception. How can you approve or certify that a doctor is a capable surgeon and never have seen him operate? The remedy is obvious.

MRS. D'S DILEMMA

Mrs. D was an exiguous, small lady, about sixty years old, with formerly black hair now turning gray, brown eyes, with limited English, a thick German accent and an obsequious manner, probably related to having spent the previous thirty years in New York as a live-in nanny with a family named Steinberg. She had come to live in Atlanta with her daughter because all of the Steinberg children were now grown. No longer in need of her loyal services, they had turned her out.

Her daughter, Rosemarie, was my patient and naturally brought her mother to see me about her serious heart condition. A rare case, and a shocking surprise, was about to unfold. I had no clue.

"Mrs. D, how long have you had trouble with your heart?" My question provoked a worried frown, a stuttering attempt to answer, then a look of helplessness as she turned to her daughter for help.

"She never had much chance to learn English," Rosemarie explained, "because the Steinberg family spoke only German at home. I believe it has been about a year she has had the heart trouble." She turned and spoke in German to her mother, who answered in German. Rosemarie turned to me, "Yes, that's right, she says about a year ago."

"What kind of heart trouble did the doctor say she had?" I directed the question to the daughter, realizing she would be our on-going translator.

After conversing with her mother, the answer came, "She doesn't know. She went to see the doctor because she was having pains right here." Rosemarie pointed at her own self, touching an area of the lower left side of her chest, near the edge of the lower rib cage, about where the bottom of the heart would be situated, resting on the diaphragm.

A different approach, "How long was she confined in the hospital?" With the language barrier, getting the diagnosis was going to be as tough as picking out hen's teeth. Knowing there is usually a different lengths of time in the hospital for heart attacks, congestive heart failure, and angina, I thought this information might be helpful.

Her translated answer surprised me, "She was never in a hospital." Ah, now we were getting somewhere. In the meantime, Mrs. D was like someone watching a tennis match, her head bobbing from left to right between her daughter and me.

Never in the hospital? That should rule out a heart attack. "Did they tell her what the EKG showed?"

After a lengthy exchange in German to explain what an EKG was, Rosemarie turned and with a wide-eyed gaze, said haltingly, "She has never had an EKG test done." She was as shocked as I. "She said they only gave her these little white pills to put under her tongue when she had the pain."

The vials were extended for my inspection. A brief glance proved the pills to be nitroglycerin (NTG), used for angina. I was flabbergasted. No EKG, and Mrs. D was just dished off casually as having angina, without any effort to adequately investigate or to prove the diagnosis. Could it have been, I wondered, because she was poor? This was shocking enough, but the big shock was to come later.

"Do these little pills relieve her pain?"

"No, and the pain is constant now."

My work was cut out for me, I had to start from scratch and seek the cause of Mrs. D's pain. Her heart proved to be normal. Suffice it to say that a barium enema X-ray study found a total obstruction of her large bowel in the area of the left colon just beneath her left rib cage, close under the diaphragm upon which the heart rested. A tumor nearly the size of a tennis ball had developed during the year's delay Mrs. D was taking "angina treatment." Nitroglycerin certainly was not going to help treat cancer. Mrs. D's chances did not look good because of the delay in treatment of a treacherous colon cancer.

Preparations were made to remove the *left* half of the colon where the Barium enema X-Rays clearly showed the obstructive mass to be located.

The shock of the haphazard diagnosis of angina by the New York doctor was as nothing when compared to the abrupt surprise I received when the abdomen was opened at surgery. I was aghast to find the *left* colon obstruction was being caused by a *right* colon cancer of the cecum (the junction of the small bowel and the large bowel, on the right side of the body). The cancer mass had managed to migrate to the left side, causing the obstruction seen on the barium enema.

Mrs. D's body had tried to "pass" the cecum with its cancerous tumor through her large bowel, as if it was fecal matter, causing the right bowel to invert and fold inward on itself all the way over to the left side, where it could pass no further. It continued to grow there in size and caused the obstruction on the opposite side from where it had originated. The medical term is intussusception, where one portion of the intestine invaginates into another. It is very rare, especially to go as far as in the case of Mrs. D.

Thankfully, a vertical midline incision had been used to open the abdomen. Although I had been prepared to remove a large portion of the *left* half of the colon, I was therefore able to change my plan and remove the *right* half of the colon without the need of making an additional incision.

Mrs. D was fortunate the cancer originated in her cecum and not the left colon, because a cancer that starts in the cecum is usually slow-growing and less likely to metastasize (spread), as compared to the treachery of a left colon cancer, which often has spread before symptoms occur, and well before being detected. The year of delay would likely have been fatal if her symptoms had been related to a cancer that had started in the left colon.

Mrs. D survived her "angina" misdiagnosis. She also survived her surgery. The last I heard from her daughter, seventeen years later, Mrs. D. was still alive and cancer-free, and living in South Carolina.

TERRAFIRMITIS

"Ya see these sores on my legs? Why won't they get well? They been there more'n a year already. Ain't no doctor has helped a bit, neither. Kin you do any better? I doubt it."

These staccato rat-a-tat statements shot at me like an M-16 rifle on full fire, opening up with serious intent, greeting my entrance into the examining room. A tiny figure of a very old, shoeless man with filthy pants rolled up to his knees was sitting in a chair, picking between his toes. The room was filled with a musty unpleasant and odorous mixture of sweat, stale body odor, and purulence.

Never at a complete loss of words, I replied cleverly, "I don't know." As an equally loquacious afterthought, I added boldly, "I can try."

His gray eyes, set deep in a wrinkled, dirt-encrusted face glared at me like a lazer beam, loaded with distrust and dislike. An infected swollen area was on his right cheek, surrounding a two inch line of stitches from a recently repaired laceration of his face. His immediate interest was attention for his legs, however.

"Well, by god, we'll just see." The challenge had been issued and the gauntlet drawn. It was up to me to pick up the pieces and to deliver the goods, as far as Mr. Folds was concerned.

Mr. Folds was an old man that life had dealt a bad hand. His clothing was old, tattered and caked with accumulated dirt and debris. So was his pale white skin, so much so that in the chart I coined a new word, "terrafirmitis," meaning inflammation secondary to dirt, as a future reminder of his advanced state of uncleanness, and its possible relation to his infection. He was frail and thin, wasted like a man who had too little to eat for a long time. His arthritic spine had long since degenerated, permanently pulling his upper body into a slightly bent-over position, his eyes having to peer from just under long white and bushy eyebrows to look up into my face. Atop his short, skinny body rested a surprisingly large head with high angular cheek bones, penetrating grayish eyes, a long thin sharply pointed nose, his features gaunt from poor nutrition and a hard life.

He looked at me, measuring me in his mind. I had the feeling he was withholding approval, his final judgment yet to be reached. He raised one bare foot up and sat it on the table edge, pointed at it with a skinny, knobby index finger. A glance at his bare foot caught me by surprise, a maggot was creeping out from between his toes.

"You came to see me about your legs, right?" That point had to be clearly established, especially after noticing the infection in the repaired cut on his face.

"Yep." Remaining in his chair, he raised one bare foot toward me, expecting me to grasp and hold up his leg while examining his leg. I deferred.

"You mind getting on the examining table?" I further urged, "Using the bright light over the table, I can examine your legs much better"

Grumbling, Mr. Folds eventually agreed to sit on the table where his leg rested for close inspection, without my having to actually touch them. Disregarding the accumulated caked and dried dirt and the assault of putrefaction odors, I persisted and was able to observe large ulcerated areas extending above the ankles of both legs, along with significant varicose veins. Donning a surgical glove for my own protection, I checked and found no discernible pulses in his lower legs, meaning this old timer's arteries were not getting blood through to his lower legs. The pulses higher in the leg were diminished, or absent. The subsequent lack of oxygen and the stagnation of his blood caused the ulcers and the blue-gray color of his legs, technically called *stasis dermatitis* with the ulcerations secondary to Peripheral Vascular Arteriosclerosis Disease, commonly called by lay people "hardening of the arteries," or "bad circulation."

His dirty, raggedy shirt and pants gave testimony to his impecunious station in these final years of his old age. A frayed, worn and dirty baseball cap struggled unsuccessfully to keep his unshorn gray, greasy hair confined.

There was little I could do for him except give him a vasodilator type of medication and wrap his ulcerations in a special paste-wrapping designed for that purpose, to be rechecked in a week.

Suddenly, he blurted out, "Take these stitches out of my face."

I countered, "When was that stitched up, and where was it done?",

"A few days ago, up at the Jonesboro Medical Center, but you take 'em out."

"Dr. Bateman, right?"

"Yeah, but you take 'em out, ya hear." Mr. Folds was a determined man.

"I can't, Mr. Folds. I am treating your legs and blood circulation. It would be unethical for me to interfere with Dr. Bateman's work."

"Now, I'm telling you agin, son," his voice growing louder, "take them stitches out."

"Sorry, Mr. Folds, I can't. Go see Dr. Bateman today. You know he is near here. I'll call and tell him you are coming."

Unhappy at not getting his way, and still grumbling, Mr. Folds left, without stopping at the receptionist desk, where instructions had been left that there was to be no charge. This old gent couldn't afford to pay any thing. Presumably he was heading to Dr.Bateman, whom I notified to expect him. I never heard further from Dr. Bateman, nor Mr. Folds, until a letter arrived about a month or two later.

The postmark on the envelope was Atlanta, Georgia. In a childish, shaky scrawl it was addressed to "DR. EarniSt Abernathy, Main Stret, Jonesboro, Ga." A professionally printed return address, Sidney Hotel, 87 Harris Street, Atlanta, Georgia, was scratched through by the blue ink of a ball point pen.

I was puzzled. The Sidney Hotel was a small, rather shabby place in a seedy, run-down part of the Atlanta inner city, purportedly renting cheap rooms with revolving doors for prostitutes, drunks, derelicts, and people down and out on their luck. Who was this from, and for what purpose?

Curiosity got the best of me. I hastily opened the envelope and found two documents inside. At the bottom of each, in the same difficult-to-read handwriting, were the barely legible words, "Sign, Ben Folds." The name did not instantly conjure up any image from my memory storehouse.

"Brenda, please get me the medical file for a Mr. Ben Folds." The shaky, tremulous handwritten, misspelled messages upon the papers drew my full attention, overflowing with curiosity.

She returned in a few minutes, "Here it is. Ben Folds, Route # 3, Box # XXX, Jonesboro, Georgia. Is that the one?"

After a look in the chart, "Yes, and thanks." "Terrafirmitis" was written at the top of the page.

The address in the chart coincided with one of the two enclosed documents, a return of a mailed statement to Mr. Folds requesting payment of a $5.00 office fee. The statement itself was a surprise to me because the record showed, "No charge."

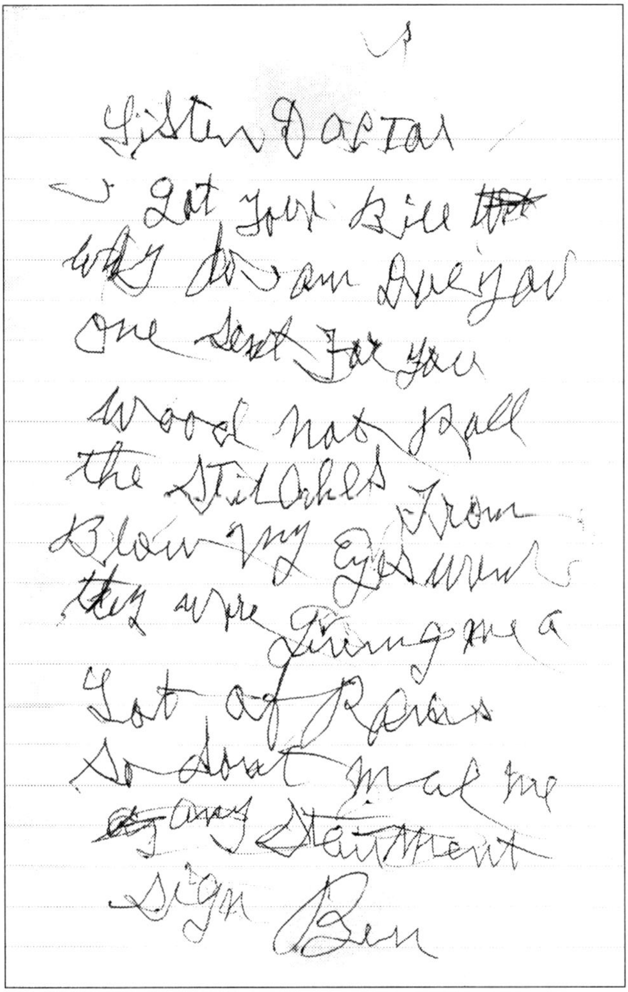

Listen Doctor
I got your Bill
why do I am owe you
one sent For you
wood not pull
the Stitches from
Blow my Eyes went
they were giving me a
Lot of Pains
So dont mal me
any Staitment
sign Ben

Invoice text (facing page)

"Dr why shoud I owe you did give servos
so by
sign Ben -----"

Letter text (above):

"Listen Doctor I got your bill why do I am owe you one sent For you wood not pull the stitches from blow my Eyes went they were giving me a Lot of Pains So dont mal me any Staitment

sign Ben -----"

Seeing the handwritten word "terrafirmitis," I instantly recalled the circumstances of my encounter with Mr. Ben Folds. His name had not been familiar at first, but a look at his record recalled vividly his case and the exchange of our dialogue during the visit. As if his visit had been only yesterday. The sorry state of his personal hygiene, his clothing, and the extent of his medical disorders was vividly recalled. More significantly however, in my reverie of Ben Folds and the collision of our personalities, was the late realization that I respected his peppery attitude and undaunted spirit manifest by the contents of the letter. Ben Folds was a memorable person, not to be easily forgotten.

Among the many axioms of life laid down for me by my mother was, "Don't look *down* on another human being, it could just as easily be you. Try to find a reason to look *up* to them."

I sent a note to Mr. Ben Folds, c/o Route #3, Box # XXX, Jonesboro, confirming that I agreed with him, he should disregard the $5.00 office fee sent to him mistakenly. The note was unnecessary, Ben Folds had already decided that issue.

His official medical record, the two documents and the Sidney Hotel envelope were framed for posterity, and still hang on my office wall, as a reminder of a contrary octogenarian who unknowingly earned my admiration against formidable odds, while teaching me another lesson about determination in the face of life's struggles. Mr. Folds may have been "down," but he certainly refused to be counted "out."

ORPHELIA AND THE WAGON OF LIFE

One of the best things about the practice of medicine, other than the pleasure of helping people, is the variety of folks who pass your way, their different personalities, medical and personal problems, and sometimes, their different so-called levels of society, attitudes, and mores. A surprise was just around the corner nearly every day. This was to be one of those days.

Orphelia was in her early fifties, an overweight Afro-American, gray just beginning to show in her hairline. She was wearing glasses, an oversized pink full blouse and an enormous pair of what I took to be men's black work pants, with an elastic bandage wrapped tightly around the left knee. She was sitting very still. Orphelia was usually all smiles and good nature, but not today. She did not want to move, because every movement caused pain. She grimaced with each tiny movement of her left leg.

"Good morning, Orphelia."

"It ain't too good, I done gone and broke my leg."

"What happened?: I asked, as though I had not seen the knee bandage.

"I was trying to change a light bulb in the kitchen, and I fell off the ladder. I believe my left leg is broke," frowning at the recollection of her plunge to the floor.

"Show me where the pain is located." She pointed to an area just below the kneecap, where swelling was seen. "Can you move your knee?"

"Yeah, but I ain't going to, cause it hurts too much."

"The pants leg will have to be cut off, Orphelia, to examine you better."

"That's alright, these are Willie's pants and they's about wore out anyway."

A large bruise was at the lower portion of the knee joint. The tiniest movement during the exam produced pain. Splinting her leg to prevent motion or movement, X-Rays were taken and revealed a non-displaced fracture of the left tibial plateau, a serious fracture. Being non-displaced, it would probably heal satisfactorily if placed in a full leg cast. I explained this to Orphelia.

Care by an orthopedist, I knew, was going to work a financial hardship on Orphelia, because I knew where she lived in a lower economic part of Jonesboro. She was also a Medicaid patient, reserved for the poor and needy.

Many physicians had stopped taking Medicaid patients at that time because the Medicaid system of Georgia was not paying them, despite the fact their fees were greatly reduced for Medicaid patients. After holding seventy-one unpaid Medicaid bills in my office for more than two years, and after multiple submissions of completed forms, no replies ever came. I stopped filing for payment and delivered care free of charge to Medicaid patients. It was easier than filing and re-filing over and over to the State for years, never receiving an answer or a payment.

The best answer for Orphelia, being so poor, and on Medicaid, seemed to be that I should take care of her myself. I had orthopedic training in my surgery residency and could do it, but was very busy and referred most of them to an Orthopedic Surgeon, the usual practice in Atlanta.

"Orphelia, I am unaware of any bone specialist that is taking Medicaid these days, because Medicaid never pays them, but don't worry. I can take care of you and it won't cost you a cent." She brightened visibly at that news.

"What you gonna do to fix it? You ain't got to operate, is you?"

"No, a full leg cast should do the job, but you will get mighty tired of it before you get well." I explained the details of the cast and the time required for healing, and she agreed.

The cast was applied from foot to the groin. When it had dried, I asked," How are you going to get home? Is there any body with you?"

"Ain't nobody with me, but I got a car out back in the parking lot."

"You can't drive a car wearing that cast."

"The car's automatic, I can drive it with my right leg and foot."

"That's mighty risky, but it's up to you, of course."

"I've done it before; anyway, I ain't got to go but a few blocks."

Orphelia may be very poor, I thought, but she is rich in bravery. I was full of sympathy for her injury and her low financial station in life. There was no one to help her to her car. Filled with empathy for her plight, I said, "Orphelia, I don't have a wheel chair, but I'll try to carry you to your car. You'll have to hold tightly around my neck to help out." Her eyes grew wide at the hairy prospect of skinny-me toting big-her, as well as her heavy cast.

Brenda, the nurse, tried to aid by supporting and guiding the cast as we struggled through the narrow back doorway, barely able to bear up under the combined weight of Orphelia and the cast. In the eyes of an onlooker, we must have looked like an odd new form of multiracial, mixed gender, Siamese triplets, impaled by a long white projectile. The doorway proved to be quite an obstacle, but we finally staggered through to the outside, creeping sideways like a giant six-legged crab—a cumbersome package of three people and a long, awkward leg cast.

As we carefully eased past my used six-year old Pontiac station wagon, I scouted the parking lot seeking a likely old car belonging to poor Orphelia.

"Which one is yours, Orphelia?"

Holding onto my neck tightly with one arm, she raised the other and pointed. My eyes followed the direction of her finger. It must be a mistake, I thought. The only car over there is a brand spanking, new, shiny white Cadillac automobile, the must expensive model of the current year. I managed to ask, weakly, "You mean the Cadillac?"

"Yes," she replied, matter-of-factly, as though we were discussing something as mundane as the weather report. I thought my knees were going to buckle from the surprise.

Trying to mask my true feelings, I remained silent and tenderly helped Orphelia into her car. I waved as she drove away.

My offer of free care had been freely given because of my empathy for her injury, her near-useless Georgia Medicaid insurance coverage, her residence location and the wrong conclusions I had drawn.

Any one who can afford a new Cadillac should not be qualified for Medicaid, and thusly deplete the funds available for the truly needy. As my Pop would have said, "Do the right thing," I knew this was not a right thing.

I see in my office many times that the Medicaid System of Georgia is self-generating, feeding itself with new people who have no business being labeled as qualified recipients for medical services paid by the State, and the taxpayers of Georgia.

For example, I had a married couple as patients for many years, both blind. They obviously were entitled to benefits. This couple gave birth to a son and a girl, both of whom I treated for simple things like sore throats or cold. I watched them become adults and marry, each union in turn generating another three children. There was nothing physically or medically wrong with any of them to qualify them for free medical care by the Medicaid System, but all ten managed to be on Medicaid for medical care and free prescriptions, having learned the ropes about how to be come approved by having evolved in the system alongside their parents.

More and more people have figured out a way to ride "free" on the "wagon of life" at the expense of the few pulling the "wagon". The ones pulling the "wagon of life" are the producers, the workers, the business people, and the employed who carry the financial load for all those who deserve to be there, but also for the increasing numbers of "deadbeats" who ride freely. The riders are increasing in numbers and the pullers are getting fewer. Soon the wagon will stop, because it will be too heavy for the few still pulling it, then everybody loses.

CLOTEELIA

———•—•———

I was sitting directly on Cloteelia's fat belly, straddling her upper abdomen, my hands moving between her breasts when I heard a loud voice behind me demand, "What the hell are you doing"

No, it wasn't her outraged husband, boyfriend, or a "significant other" acquaintance. The voice belonged to my boss, the senior surgical resident for L.S.U. at Charity Hospital in New Orleans. He had entered the cubicle which contained the bed where the action was unfolding. He was a few minutes too late, narrowly missing the climax of my affair with the fat lady during those same few minutes.

Actually, the drama had begun earlier, with a middle-aged man.

"We've got an arrest! Man in room three!" The cry reverberated down the hallway and throughout the Emergency Room area, the nurse's screaming voice loud enough to assure every one working in the ER heard it, leaving no one in doubt as to the emergency.

Cardiac arrest, already the second in the ER that night. There was a hurried scramble as all available personnel ran to the sound of the scream. A middle-aged clothed man lay on an examining table, technically dead, but still having a remote chance to be revived and remain in the land of the living. His shirt was rapidly being cut away by the nurse who had screamed. The cardiac arrest tray was already being opened by a second nurse and proffered to a young first year junior resident, in charge of the Emergency Room.

He grabbed the scalpel from the opened tray, as he urged, "Get the O2 going." The nurses needed no reminder. They were seasoned veterans, already in the process of rushing to get the oxygen and the IV's established.

Following L.S.U. Surgery and hospital protocol at that time, (1960) he swiftly slashed open the skin and subcutaneous tissue with a long curving incision, following the line of a space between two ribs along the lower left rib cage. The lobular yellow fat peeled back on both sides of the incision as the wound opened wide.

Not surprisingly, only a trivial amount of dark blood oozed out. There was no "pump" to push the blood, the heart had stopped. With another rapid stroke, he used the knife to slice through the intercostal muscle between the two ribs and entered the chest cavity. Within seconds, in a quick motion, he shoved the business end of a large Kelly clamp through the small opening and spread, making the hole between the ribs larger and wider, to facilitate the entry of his hand into the chest.

His gloved right hand quickly thrust into the cavity up to the middle of his forearm and grasped the man's stilled heart. The young doctor began immediately to squeeze the heart forcefully in a steady rhythm, emulating a normal heart beat, hoping to force blood from the heart out into the vascular tree and save the man.

Nurses were making ancillary efforts meanwhile, beginning oxygen, starting IV's, checking for blood pressure and pulses, calling out the passage of minutes, calling for more help, handing to the young doctor a long-needled syringe already loaded with epinephrine, (Adrenaline).

Hurriedly, he jabbed the needle directly into the heart muscle and pushed the plunger. He withdrew the needle and resumed kneading the heart for several repetitions, then stopped briefly to see if the heart had resumed beating. No. The cycle of massaging of the heart, then stopping to check for a heart beat, was repeated again, and again, and again. No response of the heart ever came. The time limit ran out. Reluctantly, the young doctor had to surrender his efforts after the prescribed minutes of time had passed. Past that limit, only an inoperative vegetable brain, at best, could be expected. This was the second heart arrest of the night shift, with the same sad result. The open-chest technique had failed both times. The use of the desperate, aggressive surgical technique of open-chest heart massage was being used as a standard procedure for cardiac arrest up until that time throughout the nation.

I know, for I was that young junior resident. Although early in my surgery residency, my experience at Charity had already shown this was the usual result in most cases of open-chest attempts, however, it was the prescribed protocol to be followed by all resident surgeons. Cardiopulmonary resuscitation (CPR) was unknown at Charity and elsewhere at the time; although I had recently come from Johns Hopkins Hospital where CPR had just originated, and my experience there with CPR had been plentiful.

A young doctor named James Jude and a collaborating engineer, whose name I can not recall, created the idea of using mouth-to-mouth respiration and cardiac compression by external massage of the chest. It was the beginning of CPR. The interns and residents were doing some of the first, earliest cases, with good results usually being obtained. There were early drawbacks. For instance, I was giving mouth-to-mouth resuscitation to a man with cardiac arrest when suddenly he vomited into my mouth. The man had tuberculosis; he did not survive. For months my fear of contracting tuberculosis persisted. Further refinements in CPR were to come in later years, when it would become a familiar household term.

At Charity, I had already seen enough bad results with open-chest, internal massage techniques to last a lifetime. It seemed their standard protocol could use some updating. I vowed to risk it, by using the CPR I had learned at Hopkins in the first unique opportunity afforded me. That opportunity came much sooner than I expected, with the aforementioned fat lady.

Only minutes had passed after the failure with the middle-aged man when the *third* cardiac arrest occurred during my shift as resident in the ER. She was an obese black lady about fifty-five years of age with severe asthma, whose heart had arrested shortly after she entered the hospital ER area. It had only been minutes since the attempt to save the last arrest. Everything was still in disorder and disarray. The nurses were distracted with another trauma case in the opposite end of the ER.

I yelled loudly, "Cardiac arrest!" *"This is the one,"* I thought. *"Her only chance may be immediate external massage. She can't wait. It's up to me"*

Without delay, I jumped upon the fat lady's slumped body, straddled her abdomen, banged my fist upon her sternum, (breast bone), and immediately began external massage of her chest, compressing the heart against her vertebral column and mediastinum, hopefully forcing blood out into the arteries. Good compression was an uncertainty with such a fat body as hers.

You took a lot on yourself this time, big boy. What if she doesn't make it? You'll probably be kicked out of your residency position. So what, she needs her chance to make it. Keep pumping, save her if you can."

About every eighth or ninth compression, I inhaled deeply and blew breath into her by mouth-to-mouth technique, just as we had done at Hopkins. Nurses began to arrive, bringing IV's, BP cuffs and oxygen.

They entered the area at a moment I was giving mouth-to-mouth resuscitation. I heard a voice of one cry out, "Oh, my god, look, he's kissing her." Another voice demanded, "Doctor, what *are* you doing?" She shouted, "Stop!"

Paying no attention to them, I restarted the external massage, explaining, "Relax, I was just breathing air into her, now I am massaging her heart externally." I was too intent upon the business at hand to explain further. Continuing the rhythmic compressions, I asked, "See if you can feel a carotid pulse."

"I feel a pulse in her neck," one of the nurses exclaimed excitedly.

"Thank God, that means I am getting good compression. Keep your cool, son, and keep working at the task. You can do it, God willing. Feeling the pulse confirmed that I was getting good compression. I stopped for a few seconds and checked. No voluntary heart beat. I resumed the external massage. *Come on baby, start up.* Another few minutes passed. Another stop and check, still no heart beat.

In the midst of struggle to preserve her life, I worried, *Oh, God, I am losing her. Don't get frustrated. Stay with it. Don't show your anxiety. Keep cool.* My own heart was racing, the pounding pulses felt in my head, neck and chest like cannon shots. Sweat was on my face and beginning to dampen my shirt.

Back to the external massage. Keep blood circulating and pay attention only to that. More compressing massages for several minutes. Still no voluntary heart beat. The drama continued.

A glance at the nurses showed they were shaking their heads and looking at each other, ready to give up. *Are they thinking I am crazy, or that the patient is not going to make it because the old time limit of three to five minutes has passed? I must keep my cool in their eyes. Can't let them know I am as worried as they are.*

The intermittent rigorous compressing of her heart continued, stopping to check every few minutes. The same negative result each time, no voluntary heart beat. *I'm getting tired. Got to keep going. No one else here knows anything about external massage, it's up to me.*

Without stopping, I explained to the nurses, between breaths, "As long as I get good blood flow while pumping, external massage of the heart keeps blood flowing to the brain. That's why the limit of three to five minutes doesn't apply here. In case you were wondering."

Keep pumping, boy. As long as I get a blood flow by massaging, and they keep the O2 going, there is still a chance. Where there's chance, there's hope.

To my delighted surprise, the next time I paused to check for a working heart revealed the welcome *lub-da-dub* rhythm of a voluntary heart beat. *Great news to a worried mind*!

Thankfully, the heart had started up again and was on its own now. The fat, black lady had made it. *What a relief!* I sank back, into a sitting position, my emotions completely wrung out from the stress.

To know you have been the instrument in saving the life of a person, especially in such a tumultuous, critical moment, is exhilarating and deeply satisfying. It is why you entered the field of medicine in the first place, to be of significant help for people in need. Secretly relishing the moment of triumph, I was still sitting astride the fat lady, waiting to make sure the heart did not fool me and again stop.

That is when the senior resident came into the cubicle where the drama was unfolding, and demanded, "What the hell are you doing? What's going on in here?""

"Cardiac *external* massage for an arrest," I replied.

"What? If it was an arrest, why didn't you open the chest?"

"There wasn't time. All the arrest packs were used up. Everything was messed up here, and everybody was busy with something else."

He repeated emphatically, "You know you are supposed to *open* the chest!"

"I didn't have anything or the help I needed to do that. Listen, at Johns Hopkins Hospital we were doing *external* massage with a lot of success, so I started it as the only alternative. It worked. She recovered and survived *without* having her chest laid open." That seemed to pull him up short.

He looked thoughtful, and asked me to explain about cardiopulmonary resuscitation, which I did, in order to bring him up to speed with this latest advance in medicine at Hopkins, and to explain the course of my actions in the cardiac case.

Neither of us could imagine that we would be hard pressed in the future trying to keep up with an accelerating speed and volume of wondrous advances in medicine, (now taken for granted), that lay before us during the next forty or fifty years. Many of those advances would have been thought of as science fiction fantasies in 1959 and 1960.

Who would have believed, back then, the preposterous idea that hearts would be successfully transplanted someday, or things such as CT scans, PET scans, chemotherapy, lasers, pig valves placed in human hearts, cloning, and genetic advances with DNA identifications, genetic manipulations, etc. The list is much longer. Currently, any discussion of radical new ideas for possible medical advances is once again popularly categorized as science fiction wishful fantasies. Nevertheless, they shall be forthcoming.

I slumped into a chair, weary mentally and exhausted physically, but highly satisfied about the results obtained for the fat lady named Cloteelia. She can be proud to be alive and proud to know she was the origin of CPR becoming a standard technique at Charity Hospital. I still think about Cloteelia and wonder about the course of her later life. Maybe she wonders about me.

CIRCUS MAXIMUS

The diverse variability of people has never failed to amaze me. Even as the fingerprints of any two people are supposed to never be identical, no two humans have precisely the same physical, mental and emotional makeup, especially when individual mental eccentricities are considered, as I was to discover time and again.

Today was not a good day to die. Philosophers might debate whether any day was a *good* day to die. Rhetorical debate to be sure, for no generalization on the subject can offset the reality of an individual circumstance, nor the unpredictability of the human species. For example, take the case of Henry Gentry and his wife Gladys, a loving older couple known to me for a number of years.

As Henry and Gladys chatted amiably in my office, they were unaware that within the next few minutes Henry was about to abruptly die an unnecessary death in my office. I was also unaware of the drama about to unfold, and its peculiar, unbelievable aftermath.

Henry was in his late fifties, a ruddy complexioned, overweight man of short stature, with salt and pepper hair, an easygoing manner and an affable spirit, sitting calmly on an examining table, talking to his pleasant wife as she sat nearby in a chair.

Gladys informed me, "He's been complaining about a real bad sore throat for more'n a week, Doc. I finally got him down here to see you. It took all I could do to persuade him, but here he is, in all his glory." Henry chuckled in amusement. "He's about as stubborn as they come." She smiled kindly at her husband as she spoke, and he grinned right back at her. Their easy comfort with each other was readily apparent, a loving couple.

"Aw, it ain't all that bad. I told her if I just gargled a bit, it would get better and go away."

"Yes, Henry, you did, but it didn't." She laughed softly. "What you needed was Doc."

"Folks, let's take a look at that throat and see if I can be of help." After the proverbial "Ahh," I gazed into an acutely inflamed throat, blazing crimson and scarlet by an acute infection, undoubtedly Streptococcus in origin, judging by the coloration. The likelihood of it being a serious type of Streptococcus was explained to them. A swab of the throat was taken to the lab and confirmed the presence of the Streptococcus bacilli.

"Henry," I asked, "Have you any allergies to medications? Ever had any allergic reactions?"

"No, Doc, I'm healthy as a horse."

"Now, Henry," coaxed Gladys gently, "horses get sick, too. They have to see a vet for treatment, don't they? Now it's your turn, Mister Ed." They both laughed at her reference to the Television "talking horse."

"Because the infection is so advanced and severe," I explained, "you need an injection of penicillin, to be followed by penicillin tablets. Can you take penicillin? Have you ever had any penicillin in the past." I transferred my look from Henry to include his wife in the questions.

"Oh, shore," he replied confidently. "No problem, I can take penicillin okay. Load her up, and let her fly." Gladys was amused by Henry's comment and smiled at me, nodding her head in agreement with Henry's answers.

Thusly being reassured by the two of them, Nurse Sandra administered the penicillin injection as instructed. I began writing the prescription for Henry's penicillin tablets, while Henry and Gladys chatted together.

As I turned to hand Henry the completed prescription, his eyes rolled back into his head, he began to shake in a tremor, his face turned ashen white and he began a flaccid fall from his seat upon the examining table. I grabbed him bodily, easing his fall down to a reclining position flat upon the table, believing at first Henry was only fainting, but to my horror quickly discovering his heart had completely stopped, as had his breathing. Henry was dead, dying from a rare type of immediate anaphylactic response to penicillin.

As I slammed my fist into his chest hoping to restart his heart, I yelled "Sandra, get the emergency reaction kit open." I screamed loudly for Nurse Brenda to hear me elsewhere in the office, "Get in here, Brenda. Cardiac arrest!"

I frantically began external cardiac massage (CPR) and mouth-to mouth breathing, continuing even as Brenda was getting IV's going and adding penicillin antidote (penicillinase) and Solu-Cortef (a form of cortisone) intravenously, giving epinephrine, checking anxiously for heartbeats, blood pressure and pulses to return. Simultaneously, Sandra was calling for emergency ambulance transportation to the hospital. I was praying for Henry as I worked feverishly trying to bring him back.

An endotracheal tube was hastily instilled in his airway, replacing my mouth-to-mouth assistance, using an attached bag regulator instead. The external cardiac massage continued. I was dismayed that Henry was not yet showing any signs of regaining life, afraid he was gone forever, and was about to thrust a syringe containing adrenaline through his rib cage and directly into his heart as a last measure. To my immense relief, his heart began to start working again, and slowly a feeble blood pressure finally began to be recorded. The endotracheal tube was withdrawn, and Henry began shallow breathing voluntarily. He was still unaware of what was going on about him, but it looked like Henry might be going to make it back after all.

The ambulance arrived timely at this moment, loading Henry and his IV's, and headed for the hospital. I rode in the ambulance with Henry, monitoring his blood pressure and heart, and the IV medications. I stayed several hours with Henry in the hospital intensive care unit, long enough to be sure he was safe.

Was the dramatic crisis now over? It was not. The real clincher was yet to come.

At the follow-up visit to my office one week after discharge from the hospital, Henry and Gladys expressed their gratitude for the actions we had taken that brought Henry back, and we were rehashing the dramatic event as it happened in my office.

Gladys said, rather wistfully, "You know, Henry, I just remembered, you had the same thing happen to you one time over in Alabama a few years ago when you had a penicillin shot. Remember?"

"Why, yeah, that's right. I shore did, honey. Ain't that something." The two of them grinned at each other and chuckled like two kids who had just been given free passes to a candy shop.

They were as casual about the whole affair as if it had only been another Sunday afternoon stroll in the springtime, instead of a cardiac death from penicillin, and the good fortune of surviving the "dance of death" that Henry and I shared.

At their words, my jaw fell agape, sagging toward my shoe-tops. I was speechless, as I comprehended what they had just said so casually. My mind was reeling. When asked if you could take penicillin, how could anyone possibly *not* remember such a traumatic event in the past as a cardiac arrest from penicillin? And *not* tell the physician? Chalk it up to the variability of people, I guess.

People are like a never-ending circus under the big top, the show goes on totally unpredictable, each and every act unique and different, a cornucopia of smoke and mirrors, surprises, dramas, mysteries, laughter and tragedy. One can never be sure what the next act will bring.

What if Henry had *not* recovered? How could I have proven their denial of a previous deadly reaction to penicillin, of which I was still unaware? A physician sometimes feels like a high-wire walker at the circus in the center ring, with no counterbalance pole and no safety net, teetering, swaying, struggling, feeling his way toward a successful conclusion for the benefit of patients and their problems, meanwhile dodging missiles of misinformation, the vagaries of human nature, and unhappy results—while symbolically having popcorn, rotten tomatoes, and stones being readied to throw at him by a watching, ravenous audience of hungry lawyers who are fully intending for themselves to become instantly wealthy.

EPILOGUE

After nearly forty years of medical practice, I retired, but keep my license up to date so that I can dispense free medical care, which I do almost daily as a volunteer.

Besides my "regulars," I still do as I did throughout my practice years: if I see the clerk at a bank, the waitress at a café, or someone anywhere who is sick, I offer to call in a medication to a pharmacy to help them.

Just as when I was practicing, the first response I usually receive is, "Oh, I can't come to your office." Then, as now, when I explained I meant I would call the medicine in immediately, my service was free, and they need not come to my office at all, or ever for that matter. Their jaw usually would drop open, followed by a stare of surprise and disbelief—which I enjoyed and was my reward, payment a-plenty. Only a few minutes of my time was required to make the immediate call. There was no office overhead involved, and not only was the sick person helped, but the world of medicine received a little "good will"—and a little "good will" has been needed by Medicine the last decade or two, in the face of a litigious roller-coaster path of greed which encompasses America today. The theme is so prevalent the doctor is now even type-cast as the villain or murderer in movies and the media. Lordy, folks, most doctors are just trying to help.

My spare time is taken up writing, a little gardening, the grandchildren who live nearby, a little travel, and a great deal of satisfaction in being able to still serve by helping people, my original goal.